Understanding Penny Stock Investment

Book Three for Teens and Young Adults

By Ronald E. Hudkins

BOOK DESCRIPTION

Understanding Penny Stock Investment, Book 3 for Teens and Young Adults.

Reading this book can help you discover how to effectively take a small amount of capital to create a lifetime of wealth. The information in this book can help you in your quest to make money in the penny stock market.   The secret really to the successful investing in penny stocks is just like poker and simply put, that is knowing what cards to play and when to play them.

Penny stocks are a different kind of investment than most traditional stocks traded on an exchange and it is critical to understand what moves penny stocks before you begin investing. The fact there is a small price point makes penny stocks a perfect place to start bidding for beginner investors and done right, you can capitalize on their systematic growth quickly!

Understanding Penny Stock Investment for Teens and Young Adults explains the basics of penny stocks and provides expert guidance to help you get involved right away. Even though penny stock trading provides the potential of what many call life changing returns on an investment, this high profit potential comes at a price. That price is nothing less than volatility, and to protect yourself, you must be knowledgeable and ready to implement information about how to manage your money, research your trades and exit a trade correctly to succeed.

Though this book builds you a great foundation my best suggestion is to read everything you can on the subject of penny stock investing before diving into a trade. Simply put, know what you are getting into before you click that future buy button.

Financial Disclaimer

The material provided in this publication is for information purposes only, and does not constitute advice or recommendations. The information provided in this book is designed to provide helpful information on the subjects discussed based upon my relative experience with stocks. Any products referenced or linked in the material are not endorsed by the author and people who choose to pursue particular products or services cannot hold the author liable for any losses or other problems experienced. References are provided for informational purposes only and do not constitute endorsement of any websites or other sources. Readers should be aware that the websites, resources and information listed in this book may change.

Table of Contents

Chapter One - What Are Penny Stocks?

Nowadays, there are different kinds of investment that you can consider. Trading in major stocks has become quite common. However, to invest, you need a substantial amount of investment to trade in major market exchanges. Penny stocks are an alternative for those who are interested to invest. Just as the name suggests, penny stocks are usually small sized stocks that have a lower price tag and market capitalization and always trade on the sidelines of major stocks. Penny stocks are also known as nano, micro or small cap stocks.

It is important to note that despite their name "penny", you won't find one for such an incredibly low amount. Traditionally, they are considered have a value of less than $ 5 and sometimes feature on large trading platforms such as NYSE, NASDAQ and AMEX. One characteristic of penny stocks is that their lack of liquidity makes them a high risk investment. If you didn't know, penny stocks traditionally trade over the counter. Companies involved with penny stocks are subjected to reduced listing requirements enjoying more lenient regulatory standards.

It's important to point out that penny stocks don't have a standard accepted definition as some refer to them as stocks that trade for pennies or under $5. In some quarters, stocks that trade off major markets are considered to be penny stocks. There has been confusion in some instances particularly with large corporate entities measured in terms of market capitalization having shares going below the value of $5 per share. On the other hand, we have small corporate organizations that trade $5 or more.

Many investors love penny stocks because they are an untamed and often attract less media publicity and glamour which is usually associated with the major stocks. Most of the times, the inside happening in penny stocks never manage to get to the media. However, this does not mean that they don't attract any drama. We don't get to hear much about penny stocks on major business platforms such as CNBC or The Wall Street Journal. If you didn't know, pump and dump has affected several the operations of penny stocks. This basically refers to a scenario where penny stocks make payments to third party affiliates to with the aim of attracting not so well performing companies to sell shares to unsuspecting investors. This habit has paved way for several scams to take place since a lot of dealings are done in a corrupt manner. When investing in penny stocks, you should know that some of them involve underhand dealings, investing in solid and reputable companies is the best way to stay informed and be assured of trade transparency.

Penny stocks don't involve a heavy investment such as other key stocks running on major exchanges. If you are interested in pennies, you should contact your regular stockbroker to facilitate purchase. When you find a good stockbroker, you are assured of enjoying affordable commissions and great execution to trading. One thing you should note is that cheap stocks listed on platforms such as NYSE and NASDAQ are not necessarily penny stocks. Actually, you can obtain some good benefits with low risks. Major exchanges have demanding listing requirements. Despite the fact that the advantages might not be as real as true penny stocks, they are known to be reliable. Penny stocks most commonly trade on services such Over-the-Counter Bulletin Board (OTCBB) which is a quotation as compared to Pink Sheets which is a quotation publisher. The listing requirements are retained by OTCBB increasing the levels of legitimacy.

Using Pink sheets, investors access quotation information for stocks which are registered with it. Unlike OTCBB, Pink Sheets are not SEC registered and therefore have no mandate of enforcing listing requirements. This makes them more vulnerable to scams from market traders and insiders with penny stocks included.

Penny stocks are still a favorite for many investors because of volatility and attainment of fast results. If you are willing to take the risk and invest in a scheme that is likely to give you quick returns, the volatile nature of penny stocks which causes violent fluctuations can bring luck your side. Some people have benefitted a lot from penny stocks with stocks that jump from as low as $0.08 to $8 in a fortnight. Penny stocks that issue a Press Release realize incredible results. When you research on the internet, you will find success stories on investing boards such as Investor Hub detailing how some investors are smiling all the way to the bank thanks to Penny stocks.

It is not often easy to find companies that will transform penny stocks to a major exchange. However, if you get lucky to find one, the paid outs are impressive. Millionaires and early retirements benefit from this arrangement which I must say is very rare and golden opportunity. Just like any other stock investment, numbers undergo fluctuations to gains of over 1000% in just a matter of days or weeks. Penny stocks have propelled some investors to become millionaires in very short periods of time. The real trick is getting the most appropriate stock. Despite the several risks and drawbacks associated with penny stocks, investors still consider them as an ideal method to try out in case the windfall is worth it.

Brave investors still find penny stocks a wise choice to try out because of the potential ability to generate impressive returns. Stock market investors understand very well the risks involved with stock trading, penny stocks included. Penny stocks can benefit you a lot if you learn how to avoid scams or bad penny stock and choose to with professional stock trade companies. It is good for find a guru that can show you how to effectively earn from penny stocks. Just like investing in any other stock, it is important to find someone who will help you understand what penny stocks are and how you can use them to live the life you have always wanted. Nice vacations, huge assets and financial independency await those who make a wise investment.

Chapter One (Section a) - Are Penny Stocks a good way of Investing?

These days, many of us are looking for smart ways of investing with a potential to generate good financial results. The stock market has on many occasions been fronted as one of the best channels to build your financial empire particularly if wise investment choices are made. In case you are wondering if you should invest in stocks, you need to be open minded and consider all options available. Investing in stocks solely depends on how much money you have at your disposal. While some of us may have massive funds to part with, others may prefer to go for the smaller penny stocks instead.

In recent times, penny stocks have become very common especially for people who are looking for investment channels. You probably might have heard conflicting information regarding investing in penny stocks. While some have managed to reap huge returns from an otherwise small investment, other investors have totally flopped in their quest to make an impact with penny stocks. A major question many people are asking nowadays is if it is wise and safe to invest in penny stocks.

Any smart investor needs to carefully consider all the pros and cons of an investment before making any crucial decisions. To know whether penny stocks are a wise investment or not, you must understand what they are, how they operate and how you can successfully earn from them. Many people become disappointed with stock investment particularly due to lack of having adequate knowledge before making any major investment decisions. One key advantage of penny stocks is that they involve smaller investment amounts thereby substantially reducing the chances of risks occurring.

On most occasions, investors prefer to trade with penny stocks as a way to test the waters of the stock market investment. The love affair with penny stocks is due to the fact that you can purchase hundreds of shares for a few hundred or thousand dollars. For many investors, this makes them feel like big fish. For those who choose to buy many penny stocks, a small upward change in the price could increase the chances of a fortune. Despite the hurdles one has to go through, penny stocks provide someone the ability to generate huge returns in cases where low priced stocks make tremendous gains.

One common misconception many people have is that penny stocks are traded backdoor. This is not true as recent developments have seen a couple of blue chip firms gaining interest in penny stocks. When investing in penny stocks, you should know that penny stocks also have their disadvantages. These stocks don't enjoy institutional support and therefore you should bear this in mind when purchasing them. What this means is that penny stocks don't get to appear on the screens as mainstream stocks. For stock prices to increase, it is important for institutions to provide support in order to increase stock prices.

People wishing to invest in penny stocks usually find it challenging to get accurate company information. Remember, the company that is sponsoring the penny stocks needs to have adequate information. In other words, while on the internet, you need have the opportunity to quickly find meaningful company information. Misconceptions have rocked the penny stocks industry and knowing whether it's wise to invest in them or not is based on the amount of information and facts you can gain access to.

One thing you should know is that penny stocks otherwise known as microcap stocks are listed on OTCBB exchange or Pink Sheets. One important fact to keep in mind is that OTCBB requirements are not as strict as NASDAQ or NYSE. Pink Sheets present more risks for investors since there is less oversight therefore opening avenues for fraud. The reduced levels of reporting expose these stocks to the risk of fraudulent occurrences.

Penny stocks have worked well for quite a number of people, if you are keen on reaping good benefits from stocks, you can consider higher quality stocks for investment. Penny stock investments have enabled many people to earn quite well from this venture. If you are keen on this venture, you should ensure that you know in advance how much you want to invest in penny stocks. If you just want to test out the market and still have some doubts, it's better off to start small. It is of course important to consider this venture as a gamble just to avoid any future disappointments that might arise in case things do not go as planned. Penny stocks are a good investment idea so long as you have adequate supporting information and facts on how to invest.

Chapter One (Section b)

Why Should I Invest in Penny Stocks?

It is important to know that betting on the right penny stocks is a great way to watch your investment double or triple. When you decide to buy penny stocks, you need to look for good stock investors so as to make profit. This is the reason why you need to look for penny stocks that will make bring you profits. If you are new to penny stocks world, you need to know that penny stock are usually less than dollar per share. To explain further, penny stocks do not meet the requirements being listed in major stock exchange such as NYSE or NASDAQ.

If you want to buy penny stock, it is a great idea to use a discount stock broker who has enough experience how to buy penny stocks. Since penny stocks are not traded on a standard exchange, you need to sign a special agreement or make a phone call. You also need to be careful of free penny stocks trading advertisements. This is because there are a lot of scams happening. Investing in penny stock requires one to pay a discount broker commission.

Where can you find good penny stocks to invest in? This can be a challenging question for many to answer especially if you are looking for safe investments. Due to their nature, penny stocks can be easily manipulated in the market. This is why you need to understand all about penny stocks before investing in them. To find any good stock, you need to carry out enough research first. To find undervalued stock, you have to understand the business well enough. Understanding about penny stock trading is a great way to prevent you from losing your money. In case you decide to invest in penny stocks, you should make sure that a stock has paid for itself.

If you are still wondering if you need to invest in penny stock, the answer is yes. However, you need to learn and carry out enough research on how to trade penny stock so as to protect your money. Learning how often you need to trade penny stocks is also important. Once you invest your money in penny stocks, you need to be patient and wait for the right time to sell so as to make profit. You also not forget to look for a reputable and legit stock trading company. Choosing the right stock trading company will enable you to keep your money safe hence not go through loses. A good company should treat you well as an investor and guide you through the penny stock buying and selling process.

Before investing in penny stock you also need to be ready of finding yourself in the losing side. Penny stocks sometimes usually have different prices. Some people usually see this as an advantage. The prices of the stocks are ranging between 10% 20% 50% 0r 100% within a day. If you happen to be on the winning side, you will definitely enjoy the profits but if you are on the losing side, it is good at all. Without proper information on a company financial capability, you will not be able to predict if you are in for a gain or a loss. If you manage to buy cheap stock and its lowest point in the trading cycle, you need to be prepared for any outcome.

When you decide to invest in trading cheap shares, you will also make money. However you need to know the right time when to sell your stocks. As long as you have researched and learn about penny stock, you should avoid buying or selling them. Penny stocks have a lot of information and it is a great idea to first understand the trading process so as to avoid going through loses. Although many people have made money through investing in penny stock, only those that know the tips and ways of stock trading make money. Before trading in penny stocks, you need to know that it is a risky move. Remember to use great judgment and invest in things that you can easy understand. Using a professional broker who has experience in stock trading is a great idea. However, you need to be prepared to pay the broker some commission fee when you make a profit.

Many people, who have succeeded in penny stock trading advice new trades to invest in small amount of money, understand penny stock trading in depths, learn best places for penny stock trading and carefully learn the buy and sell process. Once you have done or this, you can increase the amount of money you are investing with time and earn huge amount of profits.

Chapter One (Section c)

How Do I Get Started in Penny Stocks?

The high cost of living has forced many people to consider alternative ways of investing in order to make ends meet. Surviving on one source of income has almost become impossible forcing investors to research carefully and look for other ways of earning extra money. Investing in stocks is considered to be a sound investment idea so long as it is done using the correct approach. The stock market is complex and therefore you need to have adequate information in order to make the right choices.

Penny stocks have managed to grab the attention of several investors across the globe. The main thing about penny stocks is that you need to understand them thoroughly before making any moves. A number of people have an interest in penny stocks yet they fail to find suitable facts to support their decisions. Be encouraged, the process of investing in penny stocks is pretty simple and straightforward. Just like any other investment, you need to have money in order to purchase the penny stocks.

When investing in penny stocks, it is imperative to have a brokerage account. Setting up an account doesn't require a lot of effort on your part. All you need to do is to get in touch with a brokerage firm either by calling or emailing them. Alternatively, the internet is an awesome platform that allows clients to set up online accounts. This way, you can be able to download forms and fill them to acquire an account number.

Research is a key process that involves gathering information from various online brokerage companies. This is crucial as it enables you to gather adequate information that can enable you to make accurate comparisons. When choosing a brokerage company, there are parameters that you have to consider, this include commission charges and fees, delays as well as support timeframes. A lot of investors have been able to use the internet to find information from several stock related sites. Using qualified sites, investors can sample good picks and gather information on stocks with a trade value of less than $5 per share.

Books have helped many investors to gather valuable information regarding penny stocks. If you have no idea on how the stock markets works, there are several books out there that offer useful and handy tips that investors can apply to successfully navigate the challenges related to penny stocks. The best way to get information from books is to read their reviews in an attempt to find out how other users have benefitted from them. At this time, working with a resource that provides useful and accurate information is key to beginning an investment on the right footing. Many investors have benefitted getting information written as reviews from other readers.

Many investors fail to achieve their goals when they invest in penny stocks due to lack of information. You should always critically evaluate and analyze information before making any investments. Do not begin trading unless you understand the ropes of the trade as well as learn how to avoid mistakes that could jeopardize your investments. Most of us don't like reading investment stuff because we find it too complex and boring. However, reading is the only way investors can acquire skills that can translate into big gains and make all the difference.

When you have access to the right information, it enables you find time to prepare adequately for trading as well as discover unique and smart tactics of trading. At the end of the day, your ultimate aim is to find a winning investment that will improve your financial standing.

It is unfortunate to note that some investors begin trading penny stocks without having the slightest idea of terminologies and concepts applied in this type of stock trade. This ignorance is costly and exposes investors to misinformation which eventually leads to poor decision making.

Investors need to understand terminologies associated with penny stocks and what they mean. Remember that these stocks could subscribe to different trading rules when compared to other conventional investments. Therefore, you have to differentiate the 2 and understand the language involved when trading penny stocks.

You can use imaginary trading as a way to learn how to effectively deal with penny stocks. Keeping an account of imaginary trades in a real stock scenario allows you to test the waters as well as gauge how much you would have made if you were involved in the real trade. Of course, just like in any other investment, you need to understand upfront what you intend to achieve from penny stocks. Are you trading penny stocks just for fun or are you after certain milestones and financial gains you intend to achieve in specified timeframes? These are some of the questions you need to answer before removing any money for investments.

Wise investors understand that you cannot engage in any trade without having any objectives that you want to achieve. New investors who have no idea how to trade in penny stocks can join mentorship programs that can equip them with practical trading knowledge. Taking note of these small yet important considerations can substantially increase your chances of becoming a successful penny stock trader.

Each one of us has a favorite and the same applies to penny stock trading. Have knowledge of the markets you want to trade upon and choose the amount of shares you feel are the most applicable to you. Next, you should choose the niche industries that interest you the most. There are a number of categories such as transportation, entertainment, technology etc. that you can select from. There could also be a wide range of other factors that you need to look into to choose the best industry of trade.

You need to know how you will research, monitor and trade various penny stock shares. The approach to use should either be personal where you do it yourself or have a professional assist you. You also have to understand the level of information you require to be able to make crucial trading decisions.

Chapter One (Section d)

What Do You Need to Get Started in Penny Stocks?

Just like trading in other type of stocks, some form of preparation is needed particularly for those who are interested to trade in penny stocks. You should know that this is an investment where you are putting your hard earned cash and therefore you should make sure to have researched properly and carefully understood what penny stock trading involves. It is very unwise to participate in a trade you don't fully understand. This therefore means that learning the ropes is imperative for anyone who wants to venture into penny stocks trading.

Before embarking on any financial commitments, you must ensure that you are adequately prepared for the task. Investors who try to take shortcuts by not getting enough information often find themselves making costly mistakes that eventually jeopardize their entire investment. This is a volatile endeavor and therefore you have to make sure that you have at your fingertips all the information that you need to begin trading. Before diving into penny stocks, there are some key areas that investors must understand.

Understand the penny stock language

If you have traded in stocks, you have realized they come with a lot of terminologies. New investors must make an effort to understand the language of trading. Understanding basic stock language and terminologies is imperative for anyone who has an interest in penny stocks. There are several websites that have glossaries that explain various terminologies related to stock trading. Penny investors have to make an effort to acquaint themselves with these terminologies in order to adapt well and trade smartly. If you are not sure about a particular term, you need to make an effort and know what it means. Trading smartly means you need to have at your fingertips all the technical information that will enable you to be successful in the marketplace.

Stock and transaction Details

Before undertaking any stock transaction, you must understand the stakes involved as well as be fully aware of all the crucial details. Before engaging in any transaction, there are details that you have to provide. For instance, you need to know whether you are buying or selling as well as understand the ticker symbol. You also have to know the name of the company, be aware of the market penny stocks trade and several other crucial parameters. Without this information, it is practically impossible to trade. Please, make sure to understand all the requirements outlined for penny stock trade before engaging in any transaction.

Have an Idea of Past trends

You should never make advanced plans to invest in penny stocks or any other type of stock without first having a history of past performance. Stock markets perform depending on various factors and it is therefore good to have foresight of what to expect based on past happenings. Different scenarios play out inn penny stock trading and it's up to you to find out how trading has worked in the past. Believe me, past stock performances always have an influence on present happenings. Don't be cheated to disregard past performance when making choices regarding present penny stock transactions. On some occasions, some people have tried to insinuate that old rules have no bearing in modern stock trends, this isn't true. Investors who disregard past information and trends often find themselves making serious mistakes. Investors who ignore past trends end up making the same mistakes that have been previously made by earlier investors. Staying updated and having a conclusive analysis of past and present stock trends makes a lot of sense for investors who are keen on success.

Future Expectations

When engaging in any form of stock trading, you must have set your own objectives and be clear on what you intend to achieve. You should know that there could be significant future changes that will not mimic previous occurrences. Of course, when investing in penny stocks, as an investor, you expect to realize significant financial benefits with penny stocks. Many investors begin trading in penny stocks with the hope that they shall one day become feature in mainstream trading. A lot of negative things have been said about penny stocks, but wise investors still go out on their own, trade smart and have more access to information on how to become successful penny stock traders. Stock trading is all about expectations, your decision to invest in penny stocks should be guided by a set of personal objectives far from what other people have said about penny stocks.

Understand the Science of trade

Before declaring yourself a penny stock investor, you must have a good idea of how the trade happens. A good investor understands how exchanges work, what happens behind the scenes as well as crucial penny stock trading tactics that every investor should know. The good news is that information is available on platforms such as the internet. Successfully investors know the importance of grasping inside trading dynamics to make it in the stock trading business.

Stock trade investments are dependent on how much money an investor is willing to spare. Therefore, before putting your money in penny stocks, make sure you have a good idea of how much you are willing to invest. Penny stocks are usually not expensive considering the price per share. However, wise investors have to brainstorm and have pre-set objectives clearly outlined before making any financial commitments.

So, for those of you who are planning to invest in penny stocks, the process is pretty simple and straightforward. As an investor, it is your responsibility to know beforehand how these stocks trade, what are their advantages as well as pitfalls. This way, you will be adequately prepared to become a penny stock investor. There are many people out there who are interested investing in penny stocks but don't get the chance to access accurate information. The best way to make it as a penny stock trader is to be willing to learn new tricks and learn how to circumvent various scenarios for financial gain.

Chapter One (Section e)

Where Can I buy Penny Stocks?

When you decide to buy penny stocks, you should have carried out all the necessary research and come up with conclusive information that will guide your decisions. Penny stocks are shares that trade below the price of $5 per share and do not feature on major stock exchanges. This therefore means that you have to be absolutely sure with your decision to invest in penny stocks. If you are willing to gamble and see whether something substantial comes out of your investment, you are good to go.

For those of you who want to purchase penny stocks, the best approach would be to use an online brokerage firm. Remember that trading on the stock exchange requires you to find a firm that you can use to trade your stocks. Of course, you have to make sure that the firm you use is registered and well known for its professionalism and high standards of customer service. Online technologies have made it much easier for investors to set up online trading accounts to facilitate stock trading. So, the first step you should be thinking about if you intend to purchase penny stocks is to look for a stock broker and set up an account with them.

There are so many advantages that come with having an account with a stock broker firm. Many of us do not understand the technicalities that come with stock trading. It is therefore important to let a professional oversee all your stock trading transactions. When purchasing penny stocks, you must know that brokerage firms charge some commission to let you open an account and begin trading. So when planning to begin trading in penny stocks, you should ensure that you take into account issues such as commissions as they potentially eat into your investment. You therefore have to learn how to trade smartly to make profits.

The internet is a valuable tool for information if you are really interested in penny stocks and want to try them out. For those of you who are unsure where to make your purchases, you should begin your search on the internet. A good idea would to be to look for companies located within your city or neighborhood as this makes your process of becoming a penny stock investor much easier. If you are planning to purchase penny stocks, just make sure to look for information in the right places.

Another good place to purchase penny stocks is during a company's IPO (Initial Public Offer) where investors get a chance to own a piece of companies trade in the stock market. Of course this means you have to ensure that proper market research is carried out before choosing to invest in an IPO. Investors planning to try out their luck with penny stocks need to ensure that they choose their investment options wisely. If you are an investor, ensure that you find enough time to weigh all your options before putting your money in penny stocks.

Chapter One (Section f)

How Much Money Do I Need to Start Trading Penny Stocks?

Just like any other investment, it is important to know how much you need to invest in penny stocks in order to make an impact. We all have different sizes of pockets and this largely dictates how much we shall invest in penny stocks. What this means is that you should choose an amount that is comfortable and within your budget. A key factor to point out is that penny stock prices vary- though typically below $5 per share. Investing $500 or in the range of that amount would be a good beginning point for anyone who wants to trade with penny stocks. The tactics of smart trading should guide any investor who wants to make it big in penny stock trading.

The amount of shares you choose to purchase depends on how much each share is going for. It is important to know the amount of investment you intend to spend on penny stocks. For example a $500 investment could come in form of 5,000 shares for $0.1 or alternatively 5 shares for $ 100 each. Despite the huge difference in the amount of shares, the investment amount is still the same. The mistake that investors make is that most of them opt to invest without having proper information on how penny stocks work.

Before putting your money in penny stocks, bear in mind that they are quite high risk. Actually, for your information, they are the most risky stocks to trade on the market. On the outside, they seem to be quite attractive as they can rise significantly. However, on some occasions, penny stocks cause huge disappointments when their prices slump in a short period of time. New investors need to know that it is better off to buy penny stocks with large blue-chip companies which have a splendid performance record. This way, investors are sure that the market will be monitored and regulated to ensure that fair trading practices are implemented.

Penny stocks that trade over the counter markets are prone to more risks and therefore investors are urged to be quite careful when investing. Basically, if you are struggling financially and willing to quickly turn around your finances, penny stocks might not be the best solution. This business is basically a gamble and therefore you need to be aware of the risks involved before putting your money in penny stocks. A wise way to trade penny stocks is to begin with relatively less cash considering that other factors could influence how much you decide to invest in. You have to take into account factors such as trading commissions and minimum deposit requirements set by some brokerage companies. All decisions to invest in penny stocks must be made after careful consideration. This means that before choosing penny stocks, you could find an alternative investment venture that guarantees you more security and comes with fewer restrictions. This can then be used as a strategy to save and have more money to consider purchasing mainstream stocks. Good advice for new investors is to use an online discount broker who can offer customer friendly rates.

The decision to use a discount broker has to be approached with a lot of caution. This is because commission fees charged by these brokers eat up your profits. What many investors fail to realize is that commission fees if not checked can have a negative impact on your investment. For example, if a broker charges 2% as commission fees, you have already lost 2% of your investment even before you begin to trade. This technically means that in order to recoup your initial investment amount, the stocks have to make an increase of 2% to bounce back to the original amount. Be careful of brokerage firms that offer ridiculous commissions in the range of 50% because this automatically spells doom on your part.

For small amount investors, it is wise to only deal with limited options of penny stocks in order to keep lower commission amounts. Investors who deal with one or few brokers end up spending less amounts of money on commission.

Smart investors should carefully put all these factors into consideration before making the decision to purchase penny stocks. The amount you decide to invest entirely depends on how much you are comfortably willing to contribute towards this venture. Having understood that penny stocks are high risk stocks, you shouldn't consider investing in them if you are going to be compelled to borrow or use funds that would have otherwise been used for other key activities. Some investors have managed to realize good financial returns with penny stocks. If you intend to invest in these stocks, just be aware of what lays in wait to avoid any future regrets. Penny stock trading is a gamble- only 2 possibilities can take place – you either succeed or fail.

Chapter One (Section g)

What Happens When I Place an Order to Buy or Sell a Penny Stock?

We all want to become financially independent by choosing the most lucrative and sustainable investment ventures. The stock market presents some of those opportunities that investors are looking for to grow their financial base. Penny stocks are very common particularly for investors who want to venture into the stock market industry. These days, there are several companies trading penny stocks on major global stock exchange platforms.

Before investing in penny stocks, it's important for you as an investor to clearly understand the ropes of this business and what is expected from you. A number of stock brokerage firms have been established with the aim of assisting investors to successfully place orders to sell and buy penny stocks. However, a rough idea of the process that takes place when buying or selling penny stocks is crucial for any investor who wants to get into this business. In case you need to have an in-depth understanding of this process, the internet is a powerful tool that you can use to access resources that shed more light on the process of buying and selling penny stocks.

What you should know is that the process of buying and selling stocks is pretty simple. There are a number of internet resources that provide you with the entire information you require to get started, identify the proper stocks to purchase and sell as well as becoming successful in this business. A number of other pertinent issues should be brought to your attention whenever you are planning to purchase or sell penny stocks.

Understanding the trading patterns as well as getting full reports and daily updates on transactions can help you understand and get a feeling of involvement in the trade execution process. Before you even engage in the process of buying and selling stocks, you need to be advised properly on the best approach and financially viable methods of trading in penny stocks.

Penny stocks provide investors with a perfect opportunity to enter the market. I say this because a large number of lucrative stocks you see today on major world exchanges started their journey as penny stocks. Penny stocks are simply an opportunity to have an investor enjoy partial ownership of a company otherwise known as a share. The workings of the stock market are simple – a price increase of a stock is good news for every investor who has shares in the company.

Penny stocks are lucrative especially for first timers since the associated costs of owning them are very low. Publicly traded firms give an opportunity to first time investors to enjoy the benefits of partial ownership. The ability and high potential for growth of penny stocks is the reason why they actively trade on the exchange. The following are steps that outline what goes on when you place an order to buy or sell a stock.

The first step is to research and identify potential stocks that present the best opportunity to increase in value. Some investors develop their own strategies of trade while others use stock brokers to facilitate the buying and selling of shares. Once you have the money ready, the best channel is to purchase through an online discount brokerage.

This means that you have to make a deposit into one of their active accounts in order to be allowed to do transactions. You should then monitor the stocks for price increases particularly if you are selling a stock. If the price goes up, it's the best time to sell your stocks to earn profits. Stock prices usually fluctuate depending on several market factors, so it's good to keep an eye on them and trade accordingly to ensure you remain on the profit side. Determining a stop loss value is critical particularly if you realize the stock market prices are falling significantly.

When you place an order to buy or sell a stock, it goes through an order processing system that sets the rules of how trade executions should be carried out. Orders in the processing system are usually filled according to the price indicated. For instance, for a sell order, the order with the lowest ask price is usually placed at the top of the processing system and filled first before others with higher ask prices. The same applies to the opposite which is bid price. In this case, orders with the highest bid price get the top spot on the order processing system and are almost filled immediately. In most cases, the chances of market orders getting filled are guaranteed while limit orders have no guarantee of execution particularly if the limit price is not reached. When an order gets filled, the payments are wired to an account linked to the investor. It is important for investors to understand the behind happenings to have a better idea of how their orders are executed.

Penny stock investment is the best way to let novice stock traders test the waters in the world of stock investments. In addition to having a clear understanding of how orders are filled and transactions executed, reading and researching for plenty of information regarding the company you wish to invest in is always a wise idea. Having some knowledge about the sector and markets is something you cannot push down the drain particularly if you want to be successful in this business. Having a good understanding of future market trends and dynamics lets investors know beforehand what they are getting themselves into.

The process of buying and selling penny stocks is quite simplified. With expert advice or basic research on your part, you should firmly be on your way to achieving financial freedom thanks to penny stocks. The internet has a wealth of information for anyone who wants to have a deeper understanding of how trade execution of penny stocks happens as well as the factors likely to have an impact on the stock markets. Just like any other financial investment, having knowledge of these issues makes your trading more transparent, comfortable and rewarding.

Chapter Two

Where Do Penny Stocks Trade?

It is important to know that you can trade penny stock in different places. Finding great stock markets to trade penny stock is very easy but at the same time finding bad ones is also possible. All in all, many sources of penny stocks are trustworthy and reliable. All you need is to be careful not to land into bad sources. Over the recent years, it has become common trading in penny stocks. Earning Profit from penny stock is possible but you need to know how to trade.

If you are wondering where to trade penny stocks, NASDAQ SmallCap market is one of the best places to trade penny stocks. Companies listed here must meet required requirements and keep in compliance with the required rules to stay in the listing. This makes investors to have access to company financial results and reports. Having shares with the NASDAQ SmallCap will enable you to trade for less than $1.00. Many financial quotes and news services usually cover shares on the NASDAQ SmallCap market, this makes it easy to get information.

The ability to get information easily improves trading and invertors participation. If you are dealing with a broker, they will not have any trouble enabling your trades in NASDAQ SmallCap shares. It is good to know that shares on NASDAQ have 4 letter ticker symbols which include DRAX, IDEV and PVAT. Trading penny stocks in NASDAQ SmallCap market, you can be assured of easy buying and selling due to excellent investor's visibility.

The American stock exchange is also a great place to trade penny stock. AMEX has great shares that one can trade though they are less in volume compared to those on the NASDAQ SmallCap. Companies are required to report requirements as well as news and quotes services. This allows investors to enjoy the same benefits as from the Smallcaps Exchange. With the help of a broker, you will be able to trade your penny stocks since there investors are many and buying and selling processes are very easy to follow.

Trading penny stocks in Canadian markets such as Toronto Stock Exchange (TSX) and Toronto Venture Exchange (TSX-V) is a great idea. Most of these trade penny stocks as low as a couple of cents. If your broker goes for over the border trades, it is a good idea to choose Canadian penny stocks. Most of these companies in Canadian market always trade inexpensively because they are small in size. With Canadian penny stocks there many good companies that you can choose from to trade your penny stocks. When you decide to trade your penny stocks in Canadian markets, you can be assured of good trading volumes, great availability to corporate information, god reporting requirements, high brokerage trading fees, access to trading and pricing data, easy to buy and sell and multiple selections of penny stocks.

When you get started in penny stocks trading, you need to understand the whole concept of penny stocks. Understanding about penny stocks, will enable you to choose your trading grounds carefully thus getting maximum profits. Remember to read and review different websites before trading your penny stocks. Avoid rushing to start trading before you completely understand what you need to do and how to go about the process. Learning about penny stock trading from reliable materials is a great way to avoid any costly mistakes and make huge gains. Carrying out research in penny stocks can make a big difference. This way, you will achieve incredible information about penny stocks, prepare yourself for trading and enable yourself to win handsomely.

Another thing, you need to know that all penny stock trading places have terms and concepts that govern them. By familiarizing yourself with major investing terms and concepts especially that are discussing penny stocks is a great step. It is important to remember that penny stocks usually have different rules than other types of investments. This is the reason you need to learn about these rules that govern penny stock trading so as to make most the most out of them.

If you have many types of penny stocks to choose from, you need to decide on your favorite one. First thing you need to know is the type of market you need to trade upon. Carry out research on different price range that interest you and different industry groups you like such as transportation, technology and biotech etc. Since carrying out research is very important, you need to come up with a process about how you are going to go about monitoring, trading shares and researching. Do I want to carry out research on my own? Do I get a professional in penny stock? These are some of the main questions you should ask yourself before trading in penny stocks. A great research should enable you to come up with different credible and trustworthy places where you can trade penny stocks.

If you decide to use a broker to help you trade you penny stocks, you need to open an account with the money you intend to invest. Many people have been able to earn a lot of profits by using experienced penny stock brokers. By researching online, you can be able to find trustworthy and legit penny stock brokers who will be able to guide you to find the best places to trade penny stocks.

What you need to know is that you can earn money by trading penny stocks. You just need to have the right information on penny stock trading and trade in the right places. Nowadays, there are so many places that you can trade penny stocks. However, you need to make sure that any place you decide to trade is legit and certified. It is unfortunate that some people have lost their money by trading their penny stocks on fake sites that are full of conmen. Penny stock trading can be profitable but you need to take enough time so as to be successful.

Chapter Two (Section a)

How Often Can I Trade Penny Stocks?

When it comes to penny stocks trading, it is a great idea to learn how you can effectively trade penny stocks. If you are wondering how of often you need to trade penny stocks, you can consider day trading. Day trading is a great way to make profits on the penny stock markets. Penny stock day trading is not difficult at all and keeping a few key points in mind is a great way of turning profit within a few days of trying. You need to know that it is possible to make profits on penny stocks on a daily basis.

Day trading penny stock requires that you follow different stocks on a day to day basis so as to be in a better potion to have a folio of shares to increase your choices. When you decide to get involved in day trading, you need to make sure to effectively monitor your holding with proper outlook. This strategy usually takes time, research and money. You also need to check the process of stocks and get an accurate quote. Having a great internet connection and a computer is a good way to access your broker at any time. When day trading, you need to check your stock prices regularly and also watch the prices all day. With the help of a computer, it will take you a few minutes to get all the current prices as well as submit new orders online.

Although day trading in penny stocks is one of the quickest ways to make profit and loss, you need to have a lot of patience. The best day trading strategy involves going through a week or more without a trade since you must wait to get the best process. You need to understand that day trading in penny stock can result to up to one week gain. Whether you are making a big profit or a loss, you need to know how to handle the situation.

Day trading is a simple way to capitalize on short term trading graphs in stocks. The negative part of day trading comes in the picture when you buy and it drops in value. At this point, you will either have to settle for a quick loss so as to keep your money available, or wait for few more days for a profit opportunity. This tends to be less concern for many traders who have other assets since they can have a portion of their money help up in stock as the other can be used. Learning and understanding the goals of day trading is very important if you want to be successful when it comes to day trading in penny stocks. You need to make sure you get high percentage on your investment in a yearly basis.

Practicing effective strategies in day trading is also very vital in day trading. The first thing you need to consider when day trading is to compare to others commissions. If you don't have a discount broker, you can opt to get a cheaper broker. It is important to know that you can learn all about penny stock brokers on the internet. By carrying out research online on brokers, you will be able to find a broker that is within your budget.

The advantage of day trading is that a company rules and goals become easier to handle in the market. Day trading gives you the opportunity to trade with day to day fluctuations instead of wishing the market will rise. This meant that no matter the companies you invest in have positive or bad long term purchases. What is important is to keep watch on the trading activity. It is always a good idea to pick both the higher and lower trading ranges then carry on the buying and selling process accordingly.

When it comes day trading you need to know that most of the orders you purchase should not be filled because your bidding price needs to be much lower than the trading price of the stock. If you happen to put up to 10 orders within the month, you may end up getting a lot of profit by the time you trade off your shares.

Taking time to choose the best buy and sell prices to which to submit your orders is very important. Choosing a method that is simple is a great idea. You should choose penny stocks that are both high volumes of bids and high volumes of asks. Today, many people are trying to purchase stocks at one price while others are trying to sell at another. Day trading is one of the most effective ways of trading in penny stocks. You will be able to get good results since you will have developed upper and lower price ranges.

It is good to know that as an addition strategy, it is a great idea to incorporate hedging into your daily trading practices. When purchasing, you need to put the orders you have bought for the same stock at different prices. Day trading penny stocks is very easy and simple. However, you will need to have patience and with time make a lot of profit.

When it comes day trading penny stocks, you should keep up with the market and follow simple strategies that are outlined in penny stock trading. Day trading has become a straight forward process that only requires simple rules yet they can provide great penny stock returns. Day trading penny stocks is a great way to make profits but one need to choose the right trading places. Asking for help for professional brokers who deal with penny stock trading is a great idea to make profits from your investment. When you decide to get involved in day trading penny stocks, you need to keep up with the penny stock trading behavior and wait patiently for the perfect time when you can trade your stocks so as to get high volume of profits and returns.

Chapter Two (Section b)

How Do I Find Quality Penny Stocks to Invest In?

If you are looking for penny stocks to purchase, it can be a daunting task for any investors. By applying simple investing strategies in penny stocks is not enough since these investments are usually small companies with a little coverage and often has a lot of data around the internet. Although penny stock investment can be a bit tricky, it is crucial for a lot of investors to consider finding more information on penny stock trading. It is also important to find the right penny stock, choosing the wrong penny stock can cause damage on your account and eat up your retirement within a short period of time. This means that knowing how to limit and trade well is a great idea to maximize your potential in penny stock. You need to remember that wherever investment strategy you choose, penny stocks should earn you money not lead you to loses. To help you find high quality penny stock investment to buy, you need to follow the following guiding steps.

Avoid purchasing any pink sheet penny stocks. Pink sheets which are also known as OTC have high security risks since stocks do not meet the requirements such as regular financing statements. Another thing, pink sheet penny stocks do not meet the minimum listing requirements in quality USA exchanges. Choosing low price penny stocks trading for $1 - $2 on NYSE and NASDAQ is a great way to find quality penny stocks to invest in.

When you decide to invest in penny stocks, you need to void using your dividends. Many financial investors advise using your retirement money that you have put away for risky investments.

It is a good idea to focus on earnings, challenging numbers and analyst upgrades. You need to know that penny stocks will not make you any money not unless they are making money for themselves. This is the reason why you need to pay attention on quarterly earnings and sales numbers, analyst upgrades and downgrades as well as hard numbers that affect penny stocks positively and negatively throughout the process.

Remember to use a limit order when trading penny stocks. It is a good idea to know that putting a market order on penny stock is not a great idea since most of these companies can change their trading patterns drastically. This is why it is important for traders to avoid trading after hours and prevent just clicking sell on their brokerage account. This also applies when you want to sell your stock. When trading penny stock, you need to be a savvy trader so as to make sure you get the best returns by watching the bid ask prices. Many investors in penny stock watch the trading strategy and set their own limit order and wait patiently so as to make an investment.

Once you buy in, make sure you set a stop loss. Many investors usually do this to avoid getting into any losses. When it comes to penny stock trading, you need to be careful so as not to lose a lot of money. By making a stop loss, you will manage to protect your downside. If you are an aggressive investor, you can limit your down to as much as 50%.

Once you start investing on penny stock, remember to set a price for your penny stocks. You need to know that every penny stock investor needs to have a precise price target with a 30% to 50% gain. If you are an aggressive investor you can decide to go for 100% gains. Once you get to your target, you can leave. If you still don't want to sell your shares, this is also ok. What you can do is sell part of your portion. Although it can be difficult to sell of your stock and watch it expand, you should not get greedy. The reason of setting up a price target is to have a goal and protect yourself once you achieve these goals. When trading penny stock, you need to be careful and take your time at all days no matter your successful episodes in the past. This is because penny stock trading keeps changing every day.

Going through you stop losses and deciding to sell partial positions often is a good way to find quality penny stocks to invest in. If stocks go slowly and do not reach the required price target, you need to revisit your stop loss and protect your profit. Also, if a stock continue to track upwards and do not reach its price target, you should reinvest some of your gains in another penny stock instead. What you need to know is that not all penny stock can make you profits. This is why you need to protect your retirement money by giving your stock regularly.

All in all, it is possible to know that you can find high quality penny stocks to invest in. However, you need to be careful when trading penny stocks so as not to make only losses. Carrying out enough research on penny stock trading is also a great way of finding quality penny stocks to invest in. Enough research is also a great way to help you avoid sites that are not legit and not good for penny stock trading. Considering using a penny stock broker is a great idea to have a successful stock trading.

Chapter Two (Section c)

What Should I Do if I Want to Make a Penny Stock Investment?

If you are thinking in investing in penny stock, well this is great decision to make money. However, it is important to know that investing in penny stocks is risky and that traders and investors may engage in greater stock market. Many experts explain penny stocks as stocks under certain amount, usually under $1 per share. Although many beginners in stock trading usually invest in penny stocks, their $1 price often comes with more risky. If you want to get into penny stock investment, it is important to learn about common steps recommended by stock trading experts who will advise on how to invest in penny stocks in a reasonable way.

It is important to know that there are several factors that make penny stocks risky. If you want to make a penny stock investment it is a great idea to understand about the risks before your spend hundreds or thousands of dollar on stocks. Some factors such as lack of information or history are important to consider. It is good to know that penny stocks are not necessarily traded on stock exchange. Because they are not traded on the stock exchange, penny stocks do not have an existing file with the SEC. This means that they are not publicly scrutinized. If trading penny stock is placed on how well the company is going to perform, penny stocks are bets that don't have a lot of information.

In most cases, there is no minimum standard that penny stocks have to fulfill so as to remain on the OTCBB exchange. No minimum standards simply mean that there is no high safety to support the seller and you as the investor. In penny stock, there is also less liquidity. It is important to know that penny stocks are difficult to find a buyer. If you fail to buy a buyer, you may require lowering your asking price until it's longer profitable to sell.

When you decide get into penny stock trading, you can opt to open a brokerage account. So as to successfully invest in stocks, you need to have a straight and honest way of making transaction. New online brokerage accounts usually offer accounts easy access to stocks with very low commissions and low annual fees. When you open brokerage account online, make sure the account gives you the information that you need about penny stocks so as to make the best decision. A good brokerage account should include charts, historic prices and help an investor to make the right trade decision.

Before getting into penny stock investment, you need to have a look at the trade status for penny stocks. Many experts advise that penny stocks often have low share price at specific times. This is the reason why an investor needs to look at warning signs so as to keep off any risk associated with penny stocks on the market. As an investor make sure that the available penny stocks are traded over a market exchange and not over the counter. OTC or Over The Counter stock listings do not require any disclosure as larger stocks, this can be an additional risk.

When you decide to invest in penny stock you need to avoid believing the hype every time. Penny stocks have been a target to many fraudsters. Even though you want to make money out of penny stocks, you need to be careful not to become a target for fraudsters. It is important to know that one of the main ways fraudsters use to make easy money in penny stocks is by investing heavily in stocks. They also hype it by using less honest ways and find buyers who are willing to risk.

Penny stock expert advice individuals who want to get into penny stock investment to complete a technical analysis of penny stocks first. Technical analysis is very wide in stock market. It is very important to carry out enough research to make sure that the money you intend to invest in penny stocks will grow. As an investor, don't just trust any company management. Don't be satisfied with letting the company do the research for you. You need to be aware that many penny stocks are scam created by insiders for profits. This is why you need to carry research so as to find a truthful penny stock company that will enable you to make profit.

It is important to avoid shorting in penny stocks. Shorting is a form of bet that the price of a certain stock is going to fall instead of going up in the future. Going long is simply betting the price of a stock will increase instead of decrease in the future. This is what many people bet when buying stock. Shorting penny stocks may seem the easy out since the prices are enticing but it's not a good idea. Finding penny stocks to short is difficult but it is easy to lose a lot of money within a very short period of time. Choosing a trading strategy is a great way to increase the growth of your investment in penny stocks. Considering a buy and hold strategy is a great idea since it takes a cheap stock to keep it in your folio until the time there is a huge increase in price.

When you get into penny stock investment, you can go for high volume stocks especially if you are new to stock trading. Stocks that trade at least 100,000 shares a day are the only penny stocks safe enough to trade. If find yourself owning a low volume stock, you will find it difficult to unleash your stock when you want to. It is also good to look out for stocks that experience an earnings breakout. As an investor, you also need to avoid trading more than 10% of the stock's daily volume. It is more challenging to upload huge volume of stock. All in all, if you want to make a penny stock investment, you need to do your homework well so as to learn the correct steps to follow so as to make profits out of penny stocks trading.

Chapter Two (Section d)

Are Penny Stocks Investments Risky?

Investment in the stock market is a decision you have to brainstorm and decide whether it's the right thing to do. If you have seen other investors succeeding in the stock market business, note that it doesn't come by default. A lot of tracking and having a keen eye on stock trending patterns is critical for anyone who wants to become a penny stock investor. It has often been said on several occasions that only risk takers dare to put their money into the stock market. Penny stocks are no different and if you are considering investing in them, you should be open minded and be ready to absorb any losses that could come your way.

Yes, penny stocks have their own risks and it's therefore the duty of prospective investors to obtain adequate information and learn about these risks before making uninformed choices. One common challenge that many penny stock investors face is the lack of adequate information concerning purchase, management and administration of penny stocks. Until the recent times, it has been increasingly difficult to access information on penny stocks yet information on large cap stocks seems to be readily available for investors.

It is important to note that pink sheets are not subjected to any regulations or scrutiny from SEC (Securities Exchange

Commission). This therefore means penny stock investors might not be able to find credible information that can guide them to make proper decisions. This makes penny stocks to be considered a high risk investment due to the fact that the public is in most cases not well informed about the inside happenings in the stock market scene.

Lack of minimum standards on penny stocks is seen as a risk as many people companies are not subjected to strict requirements in order to remain on the exchange. When a company fails to keep its position on an exchange, it has the liberty to withdraw and move to smaller exchanges. The lack of standards exposes penny stocks to a variety of risks since there are no definite standards to govern the trading. It is critical to note that most penny stock companies don't subscribe to industry stock trading patterns which cause massive fluctuations in penny stock prices. These are some of the important factors that penny stock traders need to understand before investing in penny stocks. This should not be misinterpreted to mean that penny stocks are the only stocks which are risky, large cap stocks have their risks as well. However, it is the manner of administration and industry regulation standards that expose penny stocks to a variety of risks.

Before deciding to purchase penny stocks, it's always wise to talk to an expert in order to have a better understanding of the risks involved with this business. Most investors are usually misled and buy penny stocks with the notion that they are quite safe. A careful understanding of the potential risks likely to affect your investment is the first step of wise investment.

It is always advisable to be careful when planning to invest in a venture that has inadequate history. Unfortunately, some of the companies that deal with penny stocks are always new entities or those having financial complications. This makes it almost impossible for penny stock investors to obtain any credible history data. When you don't have access to a company's history, it makes it impossible for you to determine the financial history of a firm which in turn complicates your chances of making an appropriate decision. Poor track records have been blamed for investors being misguided to invest in companies they don't fully have information on.

Penny stocks are considered risky because of liquidity issues. First, low liquidity levels frustrate investors who may want to sell these stocks. This happens because low liquidity forces an investor to reduce the price of their shares until they get to an attractive price to attract buyers. This presents a risk in the sense that investors are sometimes forced to sell these stocks at throw away prices which constitutes a loss on their part. Low liquidity allows some traders to manipulate the prices in their own favor. This manipulation has given rise to the famous pump and dump scam associated with penny stock trading.

This is however not to discourage you from trading in penny stocks. You should by now know that stock trading regardless of which types of stock you purchase has its own weaknesses. As much as investing in large cap stocks may seem more secure, don't be fooled into thinking that they are absolutely 100% secure. All types of stocks have their own risks and disadvantages.

To succeed in penny stock trading, you have to know the facts and the level of risk involved before making an investment. A number of investors have benefitted a great deal from penny stocks. You need to understand that it's almost like playing in the casino and anything could happen. So, if you are planning to reap big from penny stock investments, remember to consider the level of risk associated with these stocks.

The question of whether penny stocks are risky or not is a question that many prospective investors tend to ask. It is important to have all the information laid out before making any decisions. Remember, when you choose to invest in penny stocks, you should trade with an open mind knowing that anything could happen. There are those who have been fortunate enough to make good financial returns from penny stock trade. So long as you fully understand the risks involved and are ready to trade with an open mind, your chances of succeeding become higher.

The stock market has its own pitfalls and therefore every investor deserves to know what lies ahead and how to successfully navigate various challenges to make it in this business. There is a lot of information on the internet that can guide you on how penny stocks trade and whether it is wise to trade in them.

Chapter Two (Section e)

Can I Make a Living Trading Penny Stocks?

It is important to know that penny stock trading can enable you to make a lot of money. Each day, many stocks make huge gains and smart investors make a lot of money. However, it is important to know that deciding on the stock to buy can be a very daunting task. With enough research and reading reliable materials on penny stock, you can be able to find the best place to trade penny stock. If you want to make a living trading penny stocks, here are the main ways to make money buying and selling penny stocks.

Before you trade your penny stock in any company, you need to research on the company. A great company should be able to provide adequate tools needed to know if your stock is worth. A good company should help you to compare previous and current prices. Many good companies also shows figures about stocks and registered users have the ability to see streaming stock quotes live.

Prior getting into penny stock trading, you need to understand that this trading is not for everyone. People who engage in penny stock trading always look for aggressive gains and don't mind big risks that come with the process. Before you get involves in penny stock trading, you need to be aware of penny stock trading risks.

It is good to know that many people usually get into penny stock trading because of the fast trading that promises high returns. Most of the times, many penny stocks usually have the stocks jump up to 50% at any given market session. Once you see such as a jump, you need to sell your stocks so as make profits. Using tools such as buzz cloud and stock market scanner is an excellent way to find daily penny stock trading trends. This why, you will know exactly when to buy and sell your stocks.

Use the right tools that penny stock traders use to guide them in stock trading. In the penny stock world, there are important tools such as penny stock level 2 that traders use to successful trade their stocks. A tool like this enables one to view the order book of a stock. Level 2 can also guide you to know what is going on trade by trade and order by order. Using level 2, you will have a clear view of the market activity. If a lot of buy orders are booked, the price automatically goes up. In penny stock, you need to know that the price can simply go up with few numbers of buyers.

Since penny stock usually moves very fast, this means that the opportunity of making money is very high. This why you need to make sure you are watching your investments when the market is still ongoing. Watching your stock as it begins to subside is also very important. Being watchful on your penny stock is very vital when it comes to profits and avoiding losses.

When it comes to penny stock trading, you need to prepare yourself extensively. You need to know that getting into penny stock trading without the right trading tools and knowledge can male you suffer losses. Remember to keep up with day to day penny stock trading trends so as to know the right time to sell your stocks. The most important thing is to prepare properly to trade penny stocks and watch your profits grow.

Chapter Three

Is My Money Safe in Penny Stocks?

Nowadays, we all want to invest and earn an extra income. While some make wise investments that turn around their lives for the better, others make financial blunders when their investment choices don't go as expected. As an aspiring penny stock investor, you have to learn more about this investment before putting any money into the venture. A lot of things have been said about penny stocks. As an investor, the security of your investment is based on how well prepared and informed you are about penny stocks.

Some people have dismissed penny stocks as a financial scam while others have managed to make good financial returns from investing in penny stocks. If you are having doubts about investing in penny stocks, you need to make sure that you get access to as much information as possible to make the right decisions. When investing in any type of stock market, you should understand that this type of investment is high risk and therefore you should be ready for any outcome.

If you are very bothered about whether your money in penny stocks is safe or not, you should probably be considering not to invest in this plan. These days, a number of blue-chip companies trade in microcap stocks and therefore there is no reason to worry about the safety of your money. Just like any other stock investment, factors such as price fluctuations due to various market factors can present various forms of risks to an investor. If you want to know whether penny stocks are safe or not, you can use the internet to collect more information about this investment venture.

When researching for information, you will come across various recommendations some of which could be biased and one sided. Performing your own research is critical as it enables you to make your own independent decisions. While doing this, don't fully believe internet resources that promise amazing returns as things might turn out differently.

Penny stock prices change depending on what happens in the short term, immediate future and long term. You should know that news and gossip can practically change the fortunes from excitement to panic. When you become knowledgeable about matters relating to the stock market, it becomes easier for you to know the implications of price increases and drops. Basic accounting principles are all you need to understand the safety of your investment.

It is always important to know what you want and how you intend to achieve your goals before investing in penny stocks. Having knowledge on which stocks and companies to watch can also help to a great deal when it comes to safeguarding your investment. As a penny stock investor, it is also your responsibility to ensure that you stay updated with any issues regarding your stock investment. Find time to go through financial statements and any other documentation that is directly related to your investment. This is very important as it enables you to know the exact value and security of your penny stocks.

Safeguarding your money in penny stocks means you have to be very careful not to listen to everybody. Unsolicited or too good to be true deals should be avoided as most of them are scams. If you have a successful investor or mentor who is helping you to understand trading in penny stocks, it is always better to listen to them and heed their advice for your own benefit.

With the proper advice and information, penny stock trading should work well for you and possibly be one channel you can use to gain financial freedom. Small cap shares as they are commonly called have enabled some investors to break even in stock trading. So, don't underestimate the power of these stocks as they allow you to be part of the ownership of successfully blue-chip companies.

New investors who are not very familiar with penny stocks are advised not to invest too much. Just like any other investment, you should only spend a fair amount of money that you can afford. Cases of people putting all their money in stock trading and losing it all should serve as a reminder that investors need to be careful when committing their money to stock market ventures. A wise investor takes time to research and carefully evaluates their options before making any decisions. Furthermore, it is your responsibility to ensure that your hard earned cash is secure in your penny stocks. Staying updated and trading smart should train you on how to quickly pinpoint danger signs.

Chapter 3 (Section a)

Are Penny Stocks a good way of Investing?

These days, many of us are looking for smart ways of investing with a potential to generate good financial results. The stock market has on many occasions been fronted as one of the best channels to build your financial empire particularly if wise investment choices are made. In case you are wondering if you should invest in stocks, you need to be open minded and consider all options available. Investing in stocks solely depends on how much money you have at your disposal. While some of us may have massive funds to part with, others may prefer to go for the smaller penny stocks instead.

In recent times, penny stocks have become very common especially for people who are looking for investment channels. You probably might have heard conflicting information regarding investing in penny stocks. While some have managed to reap huge returns from an otherwise small investment, other investors have totally flopped in their quest to make an impact with penny stocks. A major question many people are asking nowadays is if it is wise and safe to invest in penny stocks.

Any smart investor needs to carefully consider all the pros and cons of an investment before making any crucial decisions. To know whether penny stocks are a wise investment or not, you must understand what they are, how they operate and how you can successfully earn from them. Many people become disappointed with stock investment particularly due to lack of having adequate knowledge before making any major investment decisions. One key advantage of penny stocks is that they involve smaller investment amounts thereby substantially reducing the chances of risks occurring.

On most occasions, investors prefer to trade with penny stocks as a way to test the waters of the stock market investment. The love affair with penny stocks is due to the fact that you can purchase hundreds of shares for a few hundred or thousand dollars. For many investors, this makes them feel like big fish. For those who choose to buy many penny stocks, a small upward change in the price could increase the chances of a fortune. Despite the hurdles one has to go through, penny stocks provide someone the ability to generate huge returns in cases where low priced stocks make tremendous gains.

One common misconception many people have is that penny stocks are traded backdoor. This is not true as recent developments have seen a couple of blue chip firms gaining interest in penny stocks. When investing in penny stocks, you should know that penny stocks also have their disadvantages. These stocks don't enjoy institutional support and therefore you should bear this in mind when purchasing them. What this means is that penny stocks don't get to appear on the screens as mainstream stocks. For stock prices to increase, it is important for institutions to provide support in order to increase stock prices.

People wishing to invest in penny stocks usually find it challenging to get accurate company information. Remember, the company that is sponsoring the penny stocks needs to have adequate information. In other words, while on the internet, you need have the opportunity to quickly find meaningful company information. Misconceptions have rocked the penny stocks industry and knowing whether it's wise to invest in them or not is based on the amount of information and facts you can gain access to.

One thing you should know is that penny stocks otherwise known as microcap stocks are listed on OTCBB exchange or Pink Sheets. One important fact to keep in mind is that OTCBB requirements are not as strict as NASDAQ or NYSE. Pink Sheets present more risks for investors since there is less oversight therefore opening avenues for fraud. The reduced levels of reporting expose these stocks to the risk of fraudulent occurrences.

Penny stocks have worked well for quite a number of people, if you are keen on reaping good benefits from stocks, you can consider higher quality stocks for investment. Penny stock investments have enabled many people to earn quite well from this venture. If you are keen on this venture, you should ensure that you know in advance how much you want to invest in penny stocks. If you just want to test out the market and still have some doubts, it's better off to start small. It is of course important to consider this venture as a gamble just to avoid any future disappointments that might arise in case things do not go as planned. Penny stocks are a good investment idea so long as you have adequate supporting information and facts on how to invest.

Chapter 3 (Section b)

If I Invest in Penny Stocks, Where Can I track them?

In case you want to invest in penny stocks, you should research carefully and find the appropriate information. Just like investing in the stock market, a penny stock investor has all the right to be informed about how their investment is being utilized and whether it's generating revenue as anticipated. Stock tracking is a critical aspect of stock trading yet many investors unfortunately don't have the knowledge of how to track stocks. Some people might argue and say penny stocks are quite cheap and therefore don't require you to track their prices.

The fact is that penny stocks just like any other stock markets are influenced by several market factors and therefore as an investor, you have to be at the top of the game and understand trading patterns in order to make wise decisions. Any good investor must have stock tracking skills to be able to make critical investment decisions. When you invest in penny stocks, your ultimate aim should be to grow your investment and realize the financial aspirations you have always had for stock trading. In case you are planning to invest in penny stocks, make sure you are aware of how to track them as this is solely your responsibility that you need to perform diligently. There are several ways that you can use to track penny stocks. You only need to research and find a method that is most appropriate for you.

Remember, when choosing a penny stock tracking technique, you need to look for a solution that takes into account high levels of accuracy. Tracking of stocks becomes a useless affair if you fail to find a technique that provides accurate and timely feedback. Furthermore, the tracking method selected has to be structured in a way that allows timely updates and keeps investors informed of any changes taking place that are likely to trigger price changes. A good tracking channel enables you as an investor to be constantly aware of the changes and trends in penny stocks. Good investment decisions can only be made based on facts and therefore emphasizing the importance of a good tracking system.

Depending on your lifestyle, there are many tracking channels that you can consider. You should never go for a system that fails to accurately and in a timely manner keep you updated on what is happening in the stock market. The internet has made it quite simple for stock market investors to keep an eye on their investments in a hassle free manner. Making use of the available tracking technologies can also help to substantially ease the burden of tracking penny stocks.

Financial publications offer a good solution if you want to track your penny stocks. The stock market is part of the finance market and therefore you should make an effort to subscribe to quality financial publications. Financial sources such as the Wall Street Journal and other top financial publications have helped stock traders to monitor their penny stocks. If you are a penny stock investor, be prepared to be constantly going through these publications to acquaint yourself more about the markets. Many investors also use local dailies to find information on how stock markets are performing. This provides a perfect opportunity for you as a penny stock investor to quickly get information and watch out for your favorite stocks.

Most local newspapers have a segment that focuses on stock performance and keeping up with this information is a wise idea. It is your responsibility as a stock investor to keep track of the markets and make decision in accordance to how the market is performing. Financial markets usually provide interested parties access to their stock tables for reference purposes. It is important to note that penny stocks dominate OTC (over-the-counter) charts and therefore monitoring these charts gives you good clues on tracking your penny stocks. Actually, OTC counters provide one of the best opportunities to monitor penny stock markets keeping investors informed. When you choose to invest in penny stocks, you should make sure that you have put in place adequate stock monitoring measures to ensure that you are constantly informed of what is happening.

Penny stock investors rely on ticker symbols to have an idea of what is happening in the market. If you are not aware, ticker symbols represent the penny stocks that you have purchased. If you receive brokerage statements, you should see the name of the company next to the symbol indicated. Penny stocks are represented in symbols and as an investor, you need to understand what they stand for and their meaning. Information from OTC listings can enable you to have a live preview of figures related to stock counters. This gives you an idea of what is happening and you can therefore use this information to make strategic decisions that will help you to grow your financial investments.

The internet is a powerful tool that has greatly benefitted many people particularly penny stock investors. One method of tracking penny stocks is through establishment of an online portfolio with top companies like Yahoo Finance and CNN Money. This is an instant technique of keeping up with stock trends. Any ticker symbols you have should be added to a portfolio in order to keep constant track of changes.

The advantage of online tracking accounts is that they enable you to constantly review the prices of penny stocks every time you go online. A lot of advantages have been derived from this system as higher levels of accuracy are enforced. As an investor, you are also entitled to receive regular updates every time you access the portal.

Success in the stock market largely depends on channels of information flow particularly from trading counters to investors. If you want to succeed in this business, you have to learn how to get accurate information and at the right time. Penny stock investors around the globe are concerned about finding the appropriate tracking techniques that enable them keep track of their investors.

Chapter Three (Section c)

How is Penny Stocks Different from Other Stocks?

Penny stock trading has become very popular over the years. Many people have been able to invest in stocks and make a lot of money. When you decide to get into stocks trading, it is important to understand stock trading so as to make the most out of it. You need to know that some people have made huge losses for investing in penny stocks without understanding and learning the proper trading. Today, there is a lot of information on stocks trading that you can use to learn, understand and manage to make profits from penny stocks trading. Many people who get into stocks trading always get confused the different between penny stocks and other stocks. Well, this is a common thing, but the good news is that penny stocks and other stocks are easy to understand. By carrying out enough research, you will be able to deeply understand how to trade in both penny stocks and other stocks.

One of the main differences between penny stocks and other stocks is their description. It is important to know that penny stocks are described as small stocks which are very cheap under $5 in many stock exchanges. Penny stocks are known to be very risk but also a great way to make money. They are given by companies with a short history of earnings or history. Most of the time, penny stocks with very low prices are not traded by many stock exchanges. Although penny stocks come with low process, you need to know that their prices grow rapidly. On the other hand, stocks give you the opportunity to own a part of a company or public corporation. Stocks are sold by owners of the particular company to get funds to help the company grow. Stock prices usually judge the expectations of a company's earnings. If stock traders view the company's earnings as high they are always willing to raise the price of the stock. One of the main ways that stockholders make money from their investment in stocks is by buying the stocks when they are low and selling it at high prices later. If a company is doing poorly, then the stocks decrease in value.

The way you buy penny stocks and other stocks also shows the difference between the two. Penny stocks involve purchasing shares through stock brokers. You need to know that cheap penny stocks are always listed on stock exchanges such NASDAQ and NYSE. Most of these exchanges have strict requirements and have proved to be more reliable to buy penny stocks. It is good to know that penny stocks are commonly traded on listing services such as Pink Sheets and OTCBB (Over The Counter Bulletin Board). Pink Sheets further provides investors with quotation data on penny stocks registered. However Pink sheets are not registered with SEC which can be risky. In other stocks, it's a bit difference buying stocks. One of the major ways of buying stocks is by using a brokerage. Brokerage comes in two different ways which include full brokerage to offer top notch advice and discount brokerage that offer attention for a cheaper price. If you have extra money to spare, you can go ahead and look for an expensive brokerage to get adequate and informative tips on how to buy stocks. Using Direct Investment Plans (DIPS) and Dividend Reinvestment Plans (DRIPS) you will also be able to find stocks at minimal costs and buy them directly from the company.

When it comes to trading penny stocks, it is very easy to handle this process. Penny stocks trading can be done online and use the help of a broker to buy and sell shares. Many stock trading experts usually advise using a qualified and experienced stock broker. Many stock brokers usually buy and sell based on the instruction given by you. After trading your stocks, you need to pay them a commission. Once you are online, you need to visit your brokerage account, enter what you want to buy and click "submit". On the other, stocks are traded on exchanges. Exchanges are places where buyers and sellers meet to negotiate on prices. Most exchanges have physical locations where transactions are carried out on a trading floor. Other types of exchange are virtual made of network of computers where trading is made electronically. In stock trading, there are two types of market; primary and secondary market. In Primary market securities are created and in Secondary market, investors trade with previously issued securities. It is good to know that secondary market is what many people refer to the stock market. You should also know that trading of a company's stock doesn't necessary involve the company.

In stock trading, many people usually wonder if penny stocks and other stocks have different types of stocks. Well, penny stocks simply are simply low priced stocks in stock trading field. Penny stocks are their own type of stocks that are classified by their low costs, quick profits and high risks. As for other stocks, there are two main types; common stocks and preferred stock. Common stocks are the common types of stocks that many people deal with every day. Common stocks usually represent the ownership in a company and dividends on acquired profits. In long term duration, common stocks get capital growth and yields high returns but dividends are not guaranteed. The preferred stock represents some ownership in a company but does not support voting rights, though this depends with a company. With chosen shares, as an investor you can be assured of getting fixed dividends forever.

Well, you need to know that penny stocks and stock trading can be very similar. As an investor who has interest stock trading, you need to take time to research on different types including penny stocks and other stocks before investment. Learning the differences between penny stocks and other stocks will guide you to choose the best stocks to trade hence make profits and keep your money safe.

Chapter 3 (Section d)

How Do I Get Information About Penny Stock Companies?

Nowadays, stock trading has become so popular. Many people who decide to invest in stock trading usually good amount of money within a few weeks. The fact that investing in penny stocks usually returns profits fast, you also need to know that there are risky. By investing in penny stocks without completely understanding them can make you lose your money. This is the reason why any investor is encouraged to learn and understand penny stocks well enough. Learning how to trade penny stocks is a great way to increase your chances of making profit. You will also know the things to avoid in stocks trading. Today, there are so many places to find penny stock companies information.

One of the best places to get information about penny stocks is on the internet. Technology has really advanced thus becoming one of the best places to look for information. Since accessing the internet is very easy access, find any information has become very fast. On the internet, there is a lot of information on penny stocks. Thanks to the internet, you will find a lot of information and data about penny stocks. The penny stock field is very wide and one needs to study it widely so as to understand how it works. Saving important websites with penny stocks information is a great idea. Later you can simply read through this information later. Since there is a lot of information on the internet regarding penny stocks, you need to make sure that the information you read is well researched and correct. It is good to know that although there is a lot of blogs and sites with penny stocks information, some of this information is not well reached. What you need to know is that penny stocks subject is very wide and you can't cover it within one day. Internet has helped a lot of investors to find great information about penny stocks thus invest wisely.

Reading through business journals is also a great place to find information about penny stocks. In USA, there are so many business journals that publish business news daily or weekly. Many business journals usually have many websites that have different companies listed. This local business news are from around the U.S. updated every day with stock trading information. In business journals penny stocks are always explained. Accessing business journals is very easy and you can get them at any time. Reading business journals is a great way to read how penny stock company operates. You will also get the opportunity to find the most reliable and best penny stock companies. The fact that business journals discuss about stock trading most of times makes them a great hub for one to find penny stock trading companies. Since business journals are trusted by people and company, chances of finding penny stock companies that are not legit or certified are nil. Many business journals always go through the company's information before they list them in their journals. This makes the journals a great place to search for data about penny stock companies. Using business journals you can be assured of finding unlimited and trustworthy information concerning penny stocks companies.

The use of stock exchange can also help you to find information about penny stocks. Stock exchange is a type of exchange that helps stock brokers and traders to trade stocks and bonds. With the help of stock exchange, you will be able to learn about how penny stocks companies operate. What you need to know is that stock exchange usually plays the role as the main market for stock investors and companies. This being the main platform for stock trading, you will be able to find many penny stocks companies. It is good to know that penny stocks usually have different types of companies trading in their market. This being the case, as an investor in penny stock, you should take advantage of stock exchange and extract important information about penny stocks. In stock exchange, many companies which get listed are legit and certifies. For the penny stock companies to trade, they need to trade in stock exchange. With the ability to find many penny stock companies in stock exchange, your chance of find data on penny stock is very easy. When looking for information about penny stocks, you need to consider looking into stock exchange platform. You can be guaranteed of finding overflowing info on penny stocks.

Last but not least, penny stock information can also be found on stocks website. Nowadays, there are so many stocks companies that trade penny stocks and have websites. The fact that most of these companies have turned their business online has enabled many people find more information on penny stocks trading. The ability to access penny stocks trading companies online is a great way to find info on not only how to trade stocks but also how to choose a great company. With so many penny stocks companies claiming to be the best, it can be challenging to pick one that is really genuine. Thanks to stocks websites, many people who want to invest in penny stocks have been able to find helpful information on stock trading and finding the appropriate company. It is important to know that stocks trading websites usually list penny stock companies that they have conducted research on and verified that they are legit. Going through the information on penny stocks companies presented by these stocks websites is a great idea. With this information on penny stocks companies, you will be able to learn the best way to invest and the perfect company to use.

These are some of common places that people look for information about penny stocks companies. Other places can be found on reliable sources. All you need to know is that carrying out extensive research will enable you to come up with a long list of the best places of finding the right and truthful information about penny stocks companies.

Chapter Three (Section e)

Who Can Sell Penny Stocks to Me?

Penny stocks are low priced stock. Today, trading penny stocks have become very popular since one can make profits within a short period of time. It is important to know that many penny stocks usually cost less than $5 and one can trade them in big stock trading exchanges such as NASDAQ and NYSE. Many individual investors usually look at penny stocks as great way to invest little money to make a lot of money. These being the case penny stocks are also very risky. This is the reason why one needs to learn how to trade penny stocks wisely. While gains and losses can be common in penny stock world, they are often a great platform to have some profit.

Just like any other stocks, you can purchase shares of penny stocks through the use of a stock broker. You need to use a stock broker who has enough knowledge, skills and experience in stock trading. Using a good stock broker will enable you to avoid making any losses. Although cheap stocks listed in major stock exchange platforms like NYSE and NASDAQ are not considered as penny stocks, they are in a position to offer a lot of benefits of penny stocks without going through much risk. Most of these exchanges also have strict listings requirements and even though they do not offer true penny stocks, they are more reliable to penny stock investors. It is important to know that through these platforms, you will be able to find firms who are willing to sell penny stocks to you. Most of the time penny stocks always trade on services like Pink Sheets and OTCBB.

OTCBB also known as Over The Counter Bulletin Board acts as a quotation unlike Pink Sheets which is a quotation publisher. Over The Counter Bulletin Board always have a listing of requirements thus making them more legit and safe to use. As an investor in penny stocks, you should know that through OCTBB one can be able to find company listed to sell stocks to you. On the other hand, pink sheets acts as a system that provides stocks investors with a quotation data on stocks that are registered with it. Unlike Over The Counter Bulletin Board, Pinky Sheets are not registered with the SEC and therefore do not insist any listing requirements. At the end of the day, you need to know that you can find firms that are will to sell to you penny stocks in Pink Sheets though this is a risky platform. If you are looking for a firm that can sell you penny stocks, it is a great idea to concentrate on firms or companies that are registered with SEC for your own sake.

Today, finding someone to sell penny stocks to you has become very easy since information is widely distributed. By using the internet, you will be able to find many brokerage and firms that are willing to sell you stocks. Whenever you are looking for these firms, just be careful to carry out enough research so as to come up with credible list that protects your interest. You should also remember that penny stocks trading are also risky and this being the case, you should choose firms that are ready to help you make profits and save money.

Nowadays, with the internet, you shouldn't get stuck transacting penny stocks. There is so much information out there that can be beneficial especially if you are keen on growing your investment. Remember, you should be careful and only deal with registered industry players to avoid being duped into schemes that could seriously jeopardize your hard earned investment.

Chapter Four

What Type of Broker Should I Use?

When it comes to trading penny stocks, it is important to know that you can make a lot of money by trading stock the proper way. When it comes to trading penny stocks, it is important to know that using a brokerage is very important for any investors who want to get into stock trading. Many investors, who have made it in stock trading, have benefitted a lot by using a broker. When looking for broker to use when dealing penny stocks, it is very important to look for one that has the right experience and skills.

When looking for a broker you need to watch out for a few things. By checking trade commissions and fees you will get to learn how penny stocks trade involving large numbers of shares, you need to look for a broker that charges a flat commission. This will save you a lot of money over the per share surcharge levied by a lot of brokers. Another thing you need to watch out for is volume restrictions. A good penny stock broker allows you to trade unlimited shares without adding any fee but will charge more for large orders. Some brokers also allow a number of penny stock shares that you can trade in one order or within a day. Looking at trading restrictions is also important when looking for a broker. In most cases, penny stock broker will enable you to trade penny stocks with their online platform. You need to keep off from companies who require you to trade penny stocks though a broker.

In stock trading, you need to know that there are different types of brokers that an investor can use. If you are new in stock trading, you need to know that there are some specific brokers you can decide to use. Many beginners in stock trading usually advise using brokers such as TD Ameritrade and USAA in penny stocks. TD Ameritrade offers a flat commission structure and access to the penny stock market with no hidden fees. Because of this reason, it is seen as one of the best broker option for any one starting penny stocks trading. On the other hand, USAA allows customers to short penny stocks in market and limit orders. The USAA also have great selection and do not have any hidden fees. This being the case, the company does not charge any penny per share on any shares that are over 1,000. This doesn't mean that as a penny stocks trading investors you should not use other brokers.

It is important to know that investing in stock market requires the assistance of a stock broker to be able to carry out orders even if you think you don't need their advice. You need to know that a broker places an important role in penny stock trading. When investing in stock market you need to know that full service brokers control the market and have high commission on standard.

Back in 1975, full service brokers lost their control of the stock market and discount brokers who used to charge a low amount took the market by storm. From that time, the internet has provided a great platform for trading efficiently. Many individual investors now have access to a lot of information that was not easily available before. With all these advancement even made better by investors, people who take time to research on stock trading have been able to find brokers who can help them. Today, investors have the choice to what type of broker they want to use and within which ranges.

Nowadays, there are summary types of brokers you can approach to help you in penny stocks buying or selling process. Using a discount online broker is a great decision. You need to know that discount online broker can take your order over the phone or online. If you decide to use the phone, you will find out that they are always on point and do not have time to chit chat. You need to know that you can't any help from them unless you discuss the technical aspects of the order. Discount online brokers also do not help one to pick a stock or tell you when to sell. On the other hand, if you decide to deal with them online, you will never talk to one any of them physically. Some discount online brokers always offer access to research through a third party. They will also present to you an account with management tools either online or something that you can download.

Another type of brokers is discount online with assistance broker. These types of brokers help a lot of customers that stops short with full service consulting and doesn't leave you on your own. Most of their sites usually have more research that straight discount brokerage and offer newsletters with helpful investing tips.

Full service brokers are also a great choice for penny stock investors. Most full service brokers provide recommendations of specific stocks that you are interested in. The brokers start with a financial assessment of your personal situation so as to know your needs and the most suitable investment for you. The broker also puts together a comprehensive investing plan that you can go through and make any changes if need be. This service is very great if you don't have enough time making investment decisions.

Last but not least, you can use money manager. A money manager responsibility is handle significant portfolios which means that you should have a high amount of money to invest before deciding to use this types of brokers. You need to know that money managers usually handle investing and manage an entire portfolio in exchange for percentage of the assets they manage. This tends to be expensive to many penny stocks investors though they are very profitable.

When looking for a broker you need to carry out enough research so as to choose the best one that suits your need. Asking for professional help or anyone who has traded penny stocks before is a great idea. You need to know that any broker you decide to use should be covered by SIPC (Securities Investors Protection Corporation). SIPC protects your assets in a brokerage account up to $500,000 in case the firm fails.

Chapter 4 (Section a)

What Questions Should I Ask the Broker?

Investing your money in a venture is a decision you need to carefully consider and research. Many investors these days ply their trade in the stock market because of the huge growth potential it presents to investors. Remember, the stock market is highly speculative and volatile, therefore, before making an investment, you must find a reputable stock broker to handle your trading affairs. Many investors end up making the wrong decisions especially when they fail to get proper information on what goes on in the stock market.

The work of a stock broker is to help you choose the right company and type of stock you wish to invest in. While some brokers will clearly explain to you what you need to know before investing, others may not. It is therefore your responsibility as an investor to ensure that you ask relevant questions that will enable you to gauge both the competitiveness of the brokerage firm you are using as well as they type of stock you wish to trade.

Having a meeting with your broker is absolutely essential as it creates an opportunity for both parties to discuss the right investment for a client. Remember, your stock broker needs to understand your investment plans and goals in order to advice you accordingly. On the other hand, as an investor, you have the responsibility of evaluating your broker to ascertain his/her level of professionalism and expertise.

The best way to check whether you are making the right decision is to engage your brokerage firm with a number of questions concerning the type of investment you wish to have. This is crucial since as an investor, you get an assurance regarding various types of stock market investments and which ones will be most appropriate for you.

Whenever you get a chance to meet or engage with your stock broker, the following are the questions you should ask them. Remember, don't make any hasty decisions that could later jeopardize your investment.

The price per share: This may sound like an obvious question but has many far reaching future implications. If you are a novice in the stock market industry, it is important to seek a professional interpretation of various stock prices and how well they fit into your investment agenda. A good stock broker should be able to walk you through the process of understanding stock prices.

Stock recommendations play a big role when selecting the type of an investment. If your stock broker recommends a particular stock, you need to find out whether it's from their own personal perspective and preference or it's based on recommendations from the research department. Research reports always paint a more conclusive and accurate picture of the real stock market. As an investor, you are better off basing your decisions on well researched findings. If a broker recommends particular types of stocks, they need to convince you why they think it is the best choice.

You cannot be a successful stock investor if you don't have objectives. Just like any other investment venture, you need to consult with your stock broker and be advised on the different types of stocks. What are your objectives? Are you looking for value, growth or income? Having a discussion and asking your broker questions enables them to clearly understand your intentions and advice you accordingly. Questions you ask should be focused on clearly highlighting your investment objectives.

Putting your money in stocks is something many investors are doing nowadays. However, have you ever stopped to consider the nature and caliber of the company you are investing in? Many of us seem not to have this information and therefore end up putting our money in firms we have not researched about. The best way to know a company and what it does is to ask your brokerage firm which should readily avail this information to you.

Ask your stock broker to break down for you the market dynamics relating to the company you have chosen to invest in. After identifying a company and type of stock to invest in, your broker needs to brief you on issues such as market competition and how they are likely to affect stock prices in future. We also want to invest in firms that have a bright future and good prospects, make sure to ask your stock representative whether the company you plan to invest in is a market leader, middle player or a new market entrant. This information is critical for you as an investor as you need to be assured of where you are investing your money.

Questions on issues such as company earnings and revenue history must be addressed because it is information that you need to know before putting your money in stocks. There are several financial indicators that can be used to judge the level of company performance. A stock broker might be best placed to give advice based on the facts and figures and present this information in a simplified manner that is easy to comprehend. So, make sure to ask questions particularly to gauge the level of how well a company is performing financially.

The issue of dividends is quite a hot topic in the stock investment industry. A dividend is the amount paid when a business makes profits and decides to reward its shareholders. Various companies have various dividend structures and it is therefore good to inquire from your stock broker if the company you intend to invest in pays dividends to its shareholders.

Other critical issues such as price earnings ratio and projected growth rates should be provided by the stock broker and clearly interpreted to enable an investor make wise decisions.

Remember, when you visit a stock brokerage firm, you should ask as many questions as possible. It is only with proper and accurate information that you can be able to make sound investment decisions. The stock market industry has a lot of potential but only for those who make investments after critically analyzing information.

Chapter 4 (Section b)

What Options Does My Broker Have for Executing My Trade?

Most of us take interest in stock trading yet we don't fully understand how what happens when actual trading takes place. This applies to traders as well who may not fully comprehend the steps and procedures required to execute trading. Ordinarily, this responsibility is left in the hands of the stock broker who is charged with the responsibility of filling an order. Most of us think orders are completed immediately we click "enter" to begin the transaction. It is quite fascinating to note that a lot happens once an order is filled in terms of exploring various possibilities that can be used to execute the trade. It is important to note that issues of time delays as well as the location and procedure of order execution will determine the transaction charges and value of the stock.

Many investors mistakenly think that online trading accounts directly connect them to the securities markets, however this is not true. What happens is when an investor requests a trade, the order is not forwarded to the securities market. Instead, a broker receives the order and evaluates the available best options to deal with the execution. Please note that all investor trade orders are received by a broker regardless of whether they were placed online or through the phone.

Note that there are a number of methods a broker can use to fill your order:

- Order to the Floor: A broker has the freedom to send your order to the floor of a stock exchange platform. This happens on major platforms such as New York Stock Exchange (NYSE). The other option is to send the order to regional exchanges. In this case, a fee called payment for order flow is paid by the regional exchange to a broker as a privilege to be allowed to execute a broker's order. Sending orders to the floor usually takes time as the broker has to physically fill in the order which could take some time.

- Order to Third Market Maker: Besides sending orders directly to the floor for trade execution, your broker can process your orders using a third market maker. In most cases, using this method becomes an option if the broker is convinced with a good offer likely to give them a good incentive. In this case, the broker may decide to leave the order in the hands of the third market maker. Another option is when the broker has no membership in the exchange the order should be executed. This then forces a broker to
seek the services of a third market maker to present the order on their behalf.

- Internalization: In this case, the broker uses the available stocks in possession of your brokerage firm to fill out pending orders for trade execution. The main advantage of this approach is that it takes a very short time for the order to be executed.

- Electronic Communications Network (ECN) – Technology has played a major role in facilitating online stock trading. ECNs as they are commonly referred to basically match sell and buy orders. These systems work very well with limit orders because of their capability to quickly match prices.

- Order to Market Maker: This option happens for OTC markets such as NASDAQ. In this case, your broker sends your trade orders to a market maker who is usually the administrator of the stock you wish to purchase or sell. Many brokers love this option because it allows them to make some extra money on the transaction by charging a lucrative payment for order flow fee. The only downside of this process is that the broker might approach a market maker who offers them the best incentive at the expense of the type of quality of stock.

From the above options, you can clearly see that the options a broker chooses to execute your trade are based entirely on the motives they have and what they wish to achieve. It is human nature that the broker may also be interested on making maximum profit from your order and this may incline them to options they feel will benefit them the most. Sometimes, this is a risk for you as an investor as broker may concentrate on making their own profits and forget the core value of the transaction which is to find for you the best quality type of stock. Regional exchange and third market maker are the most lucrative options for brokers since they allow them to gain from payment for order flow.

The good news is that as an investor, you have the right to place certain limitations that guard you from unscrupulous brokers who are out only make profits when executing your trades. Brokers are obliged within confines of the law to make sure that investors benefit from the best order execution channels. However, looking at it from both perspectives, brokers are also on their part doing business and therefore want to engage in transactions that will earn them revenue.

Research has indicated that most brokers try to execute trades in a manner that will best benefit their clients while at the same time benefit from goodies that arise out of the transaction. The good news is that Securities and Exchange Commission (SEC) has been set up to ensure that investor interests are given top priority.

The SEC has policies in place to protect investors and ensure that brokers ply their trade within a defined legal framework that makes them accountable to their clients. The aim here is to achieve the best execution for the benefit of an investor. In this case, brokers are required to provide regular reports indicating the quality of executions per stock. The reporting also includes how market orders are dealt with as well as a comparison between the execution prices and public quote effective spreads.

With such measures in place, the SEC has an easier time monitoring brokers to know brokers who are trading ethically with the investor's interest as a priority and those who are only interested in making profits. Furthermore, SEC law requires brokers to notify investors once per week in case their orders have not been send for the best execution.

The methodology used for order execution is very important becomes it determines the outcome of the transaction. The nature of circumstances under which the order is placed for execution as well as the type of order determines the direction the transaction will follow. For example when placing a limit order, your risk is your order not being filled as opposed to market order where speed and price become the main factors determining the nature of execution.

Chapter 4 (Section c)

What Questions Should I Ask About the Progress of My Penny Stock Investments?

When you make an investment in penny stocks or any other venture, it is critical to keep an eye on your investment to see whether you are making any gains or not. Some investors leave the responsibility of monitoring their stocks to brokers. This is not wise enough as you need to have a more proactive role in safeguarding your investment. There is so much information and therefore you shouldn't entirely depend on experts to give you even the obvious information that can otherwise find out for yourself.

The main reason why you are in this venture is to grow your penny stock investment and therefore it's natural to want to know what is happening. The questions you ask about your penny stock investment basically narrow down to what solutions are available for monitoring your penny stocks on the market. There are several factors and events that shape the price of penny stocks and therefore having prior information on how this is likely to impact on your investment cannot be underscored. Technology has played a large role in helping to demystifying complex financial information into simple formats that can be easily interpreted by the public.

Some of us choose to invest in penny stocks for shorter periods of time while others treat this investment as a long term venture. It doesn't matter your goals for investment, the underlying factor is the need to remain informed and updated on your investment. If you have any questions regarding your investment, you should have them addressed by your brokerage firm or alternatively, use the internet to research and educate yourself more on how to become a better manager of your investment.

The first critical question that you need to find out is the price of penny stock and the ranges within which the price is likely to shift. This is important because truth be said, nobody wants to venture into a loss making venture that leaves them in a worse off financial position. Large cap companies traditionally have more predictable revenue and earnings structures. This then makes it much easier to factor in company operations in relation to share prices. For the case of penny stocks, calculating the real worth of the stocks can be challenging because of the absence of a proven product, lack of inventories and revenue stream.

If you are dealing with penny stocks, you should know that their price is highly speculative so knowing the real value can be quite tricky. However, by observing the history of how these stocks have performed in the past, industry experts would have some useful insights into the value and predictability of the share price. This is information they can share with you if you inquire more about penny stock prices and their implications. Asking questions regarding price is very important because this is the cornerstone of your investment. While it is important to know the actual worth of your stocks, asking questions regarding pricing structures could give you useful pointers.

Just like earlier mentioned, speculation is highly associated with penny stocks. This is due to the fact that most of the companies dealing with penny stocks have little information on the public stop, lack of defined management structures as well as lack of enough information on revenue streams. As an investor, it is important to ask questions that related to speculation of markets and the impact this will have on your penny stock investment. When trading in penny stocks, you might not be able to make lots of money but get a satisfactory return on your investment. It all depends on what is happening on the market and how this will trickle down to affect the unit share price of penny stocks.

The issue of risk tolerance is usually downplayed but has a lot of significance particularly when you are dealing with penny stocks. It is important to note that given the risk of trading these stocks, you need to be briefed and made to understand what the likely implications are when your investment is faced with different types of risks and what decisions you need to take. An expert has the capability to explain to you how as an investor you need to safeguard your investment and ensure that the level of risk facing your penny stock doesn't jeopardize your investment.

The availability of information is very important for anyone who has an investment in the stock market. The only way you can know how your stocks are faring is having access to numerous information platforms that inform you about major events happening in the industry. Before putting your money into the stock market, it is good to inquire about the availability of information sources. Factors such as accuracy, reliability and consistency of these channels are some of the questions you as an investor need to get clarification on. It's quite stressful to manage an investment you cannot access updates and any important information that you might need to know.

Every penny stock needs to understand Spread and what it means. This is the difference between bid price and ask price is usually referred to as Spread. Every stock investor including those dealing with penny stocks need to have adequate information and understand what this means and how to interpret various values on the market.

The internet has several information platforms where investors can get their questions answered on penny stocks. To succeed as a penny stock investor, you must embrace research and ask as many questions as possible to get a sense of knowing what is happening to your investment. Asking some of these questions puts you in a better position to understand any undertakings you take while trading your penny stocks. We are all looking for investment ventures that will contribute to our financial success. However, success only comes to those who diligently seek information and use it wisely to ensure the expansion of their investment. Don't assume to ask any question as the most insignificant of questions could turn out to be the most important.

Chapter 4 (Section d)

What is the Brokers Mark Up or Mark Down?

In stock market, you will have come across the terms markup and markdown. Well, markdown simply refers to the negative spread that takes between the prices a broker charges a client for a security and the highest price at which this security is sold between brokers. The markup is the opposite of markdown. In simple terms, markup is the difference between the cost of a product and its selling price. The markup can also be explained as the fixed amount or a percentage of the selling price.

How does markdown/markup work? If a broker wants to increase their sales in a security, he will have to choose to sell them at a markdown price. In other words, if a broker sells a security to a client at cheap lower than the higher bid selling price in the securities market among brokers, the price is known as the markdown price. It is important to understand the difference between the markdown and markup because markup is the positive spread between the lowest bid price in the broker market and the higher price a broker charges the clients. Both the markdown and markup are important to a broker because they motivate the broker to sell securities at markdown prices among clients in hope to get multiple commissions at a higher sales volume to offset money lost in the negative spread.

The markup/markdown offers many benefits in terms of calculation. It makes it easy to determine the production cost. One of the main advantages is that throughout the time of increasing cost, the markup/markdown helps to keep off inflation effects. When costs decline, this markup/markdown affects cost charges. Many businesses which implement markup/markdown technique pass all the production costs to the customers and generate profit.

Nowadays, markups /markdown have become a great concern to many regulators. The brokerage firm markup/markdown policies and process are under strict supervision from NASD and SEC. It is good to know that markup or markdown is the amount of money that is in the market that a broker dealer charges to customers on a trade. When it comes to trading, the inside market has the highest bid price and lowest ask price. Bid price is the price at which the market will buy the securities from a customer. The lowest ask price is the price at which the market will sell the stock to a potential customer. You need to know that the different between the bid and the ask price is known as the spread.

In NASD Policy exaggerating the prices in markup is a violation of both the NASD's markup policy. The NASD policy indicates that the markup/mark down which is over 5% above the operating market price to be a violation of the requirements. Sometimes, unavoidable circumstances can affect the markup/markdown of over 5%, such markup/markdown require compliance department approval before such charges are made.

The SEC rule usually views markup/markdown that is over 10% above the operating market price. The NASD board of governors has indicated that a 5% is a guide not rule and that a member may not justify markup on the basis on expenses which are exaggerated. The markup/markdown in the operating market price is an important aspect in determining fairness when it comes to dealing with customers in transactions. In a market where a member controls the market they own the rights of cost in the best indication in the prevailing market.

However, it is important to consider some factors such as the type of security involved, availability of the security in the prevailing market, the price of the security, amount of money in a given transaction, disclosure, the pattern of markups and the nature of the member's business.

When it comes to markup/markdown, you have to learn their pattern in domination and control in the market. At times, markup cause concerns especially when the broker or dealer dominates the market for a specific security. In such circumstances, the inside market is controlled by the broker's contemporaneous cost and not the market quotes.

It is good to know that using the contemporaneous cost can have an effect on the amount of markup. Nowadays, brokerage firms are carefully monitoring the firm's market to ensure that traders are aware of when the firm is ready to control the market. In order to monitor the firm activities, a lot of brokerage firms form and monitor in house domination and control charts. A brokerage firm domination chart is simply set on a weekly basis and securities in the brokerage firm that makes a market have a certain percentage determined for each security. The domination percentage will be determined by a numerator that comprises a number of shares in a particular security traded by the brokerage firm and its potential customers separated by a denominator of the volume of shares traded as reported by NASDAQ.

The brokerage firm controls the chart and is set forth on a monthly basis. A control percentage is determined by a numerator comprised of a total number of shares held within the time a brokerage firm is reviewing trading accounts and the accounts of its customers divided by a denominator. Although most of these control and domination charts do not guarantee free trading room, these documentations help to prevent any violation and provide a defense in case of a regulatory action. It is important to know that SROs use these charts and procedures to monitor markup/markdown issues, brokerage firms as well as advise traders to ensure that these procedures are put in place.

It is also important to know that there are different types of broker client markups. For each currency a broker can choose one of the free per trade client markup from minimum amount, maximum amount, ticket charge, absolute markup and absolute amount, % Markup and exchange regulatory fees. When it comes to markup, brokers can view commission markup schedules of their client accounts on the markup summary in account management.

Chapter 4 (Section e)

Who Are Market Makers?

Most of the time, stock traders always wonder who is likely to buy from them when they decide to sell. In the liquid market, there is always someone willing to sell stock when you are buying and someone willing to buy stock when you are selling. However, you need to know that there are times that nobody wants to buy when you are selling and vice versa, this is where market makers come in.

It is important to know that a market maker can be a representative or individual whose main function it to help in making of the market in options exchange by making bids and offering his account in absence of public buy and sell orders to guarantee market transaction are handled the best way possible.

When an option trader puts an order to buy a stock option which no one wants to sell, the market maker sells that stock option to the option trader from listed in their folio. If an option trader places an order to sell a stock option which no one wants to purchase, the market makers buy the stock option from option trader. By doing so, the market orders continuous moving by removing sudden ditched found in buying and selling process.

Market makers companies such as NASDAQ or OTC (over the market) are commonly used by many stock traders. You need to note that all transactions usually pass through one market maker and next to another. In the market maker system, market makers usually compete with another buy and sell stocks options to investors by showing quotes and requested to buy and sell at displayed bids and offers. It is good to note that an investor can be dealing with different market makers immediately an investor places order which cannot be filled by the inventory. Normally, market makers act as the "actual market". When a stock trader places an order with a broker, the broker fills the order by either buying or selling with the Market Makers.

It is important to know that market maker system comes with a lot of advantages. In Market Maker system many market makers have be signed to security. This improves overall liquidity and makes market manipulation more difficult.

You need to know that market makers have given options traders a negative picture as people who purchase at low prices and sell at high prices especially when an option trader is desperate to buy or sell a position. If you were to remove market makers from the market, prices of selling and buying the stocks can extremely become very high. Also you could end up losing a lot of money because you will be forced to sell your stocks at a throw away price that a buyer wants. As you can see, in cases of imbalanced buying and selling situation, the market makers play a very vital role of creating liquidity for prices in between so as to get rid of huge gaps and maintain liquid market for all.

Market Makers usually don't get paid any commission to buy and sell stock options. This usually leaves many traders wondering how they make their profits. Well, many institutional market makers usually earn a salary from the market maker firm that they present. Some market makers companies such as Morgan Stanley usually commit their own capital to maintain an inventory of stocks and options and represent custom orders. On the trading ground, market maker s usually makes money by maintaining a difference between the price they would buy and the price they will sell on a particular stock option. This difference in price is usually known as Bid or Ask spread. You need to know that a bid or ask spread usually makes sure that an order to buy and an order to sell is reached the right way. At the end, market maker makes the difference in Bid and Ask Spread as profit.

You need to know that when a market maker is not really confident that a stock or stock option can be immediately bought and sold. The fact that very few option traders have security, then there is risk for the stock option traders and the Market Maker buys can be sold when the market price lowers than the existing price therefore leading to a loss. In order to prevent such risk, Market Makers usually widen the bid and ask spread so that the transaction remains risk free over the larger price range.

Market Makers are simply buying and selling stocks and stock options. This also means that market makers are usually exposed to different types of risks. Most of the time, Market Makers usually end up owning stocks or stocks options and this usually expose them to directional risk. This enhanced Market Makers to protect themselves from direct risks through use of synthetic positions. A market maker's position way particularly in making markets for stocks options is very complex and requires calculation and execution. The fact that market makers are complex in handling different kinds of risks , this makes new market makers lose money to the market despite the privileges of being a market maker.

If you are wondering how you can become a market maker, you need to know that you can achieve this by joining one of the Market Maker companies such as Goldman Sachs or better still using a clearing agency or brokerage firm which is a member of NASDAQ. Most of this companies or firms always provide job training and requires all applicants to a bachelor's degree and excellent numeracy and analytical skills.

Many market maker companies also have entry examinations in order to make sure that applicants have numeracy and analytical skills. For a fact, being a market maker requires a lot of more than just being good with mathematics as it also requires more mental strength to be a market maker. Another way you can become a market maker is by owning a trading pit in NASDAQ which can be a bit difficult to some people.

Chapter 4 (Section f)

What Are Market Makers?

It is important to note that people do not really understand the ability to buy and sell stocks within the required duration. By simply placing an order with your broker, you will sell your stocks fast. As an investor, do you ever wonder how stock trading is made possible? Each time an investment is sold or bought there is always someone on the other end of the transaction. For instance, if you wanted to purchase 1000 shares of a particular company, you are required to look for a willing seller and vice versa.

Chances of finding a person who is interested in buying or selling the same number of shares of the same company at the same time are very minimal. You should know that a market maker is a bank or brokerage company that is always ready for trading session with ask and bid price. This is an advantage for you since you can be able to place an order to sell your many shares of a specific company. A market maker will then buy the stocks from you.

It is important to know that market makers compete for customer order by presenting buy and sell quotations for an assured number of shares. The only difference between the price at which the market maker is ready to buy a security and the price at which a company is willing to sell is known as the market maker spread. Since each market maker can buy or sell a stock at any time they want, the market maker spread represents the market maker profits on each given trade.

You need to know that once an order has been received, the market maker instantly sells from its own inventory or looks for an offsetting order. An offsetting order can be anywhere from 4 to 40 or even more for market makers for a specific stock depending on the average daily volume. As an investor, you need to know that market makers play an important role in the secondary market especially in enhancing stock liquidity and promoting long term growth in the market.

It is important to know that market makers should contain two sided quotes i.e. bid and ask within a specified spread. A market is created when the chosen market maker quotes bids and offers for a longer duration. Market maker ensures that there is a buyer for every sell order and for buy order at the same time. After the market maker has announced a price, one is required to buy or sell at least 1,000 securities at the advertised price. Once the market maker has bought or sold these shares, one may go ahead and `leave the market' and enter a new bid or request for a price to make profit on the previous trade.

When it comes to market makers buying and selling repeatedly with large order sizes can definitely provide good profits. At the end of the day, market makers do this to provide liquidity to individual and institutional investors. One the main risk for market maker is the amount of time that is spent between two transactions. You need to know that the faster one make the spread the money the market maker has the ability to make.

You need to know that making money from difference in bid and ask prices is not the only important aspect in market makers. One of the main roles is to provide liquidity to company's clients from which they will receive commission. Market makers also help in facilitating trade for other brokerage companies which have similar duties of a specialist. It is good to note that market makers are expected by law to give customers the best bid and ask for every market order transaction. This helps to guarantee fair and reasonable two sided market. In case these rules and guidance are not followed, the customer's profits will be at risk and share prices will be more volatile.

As an investor, you should know that NASDAQ is one of the best examples of Market Makers. NASDAQ has more than 500 members firms and companies and act as Nasdaq market makers thus keeping the financial markets running effectively since they are always willing to quote both bid and price on an asset.

It is good to know that market makers should be compensated for all the risk they go through. For instance, Market Makers can make loses after they have purchased your stocks. To prevent this, the market makers need to maintain a spread on their stock they cover. For instance, if the market maker buys your shares from you for $100 at the asking price and then sell them to a buyer at $100.05 at a biding price. The difference between the asking price is only $.05 but due to the fact that they trade millions of shares in a day, they manage to go home with a lot of money thus get extra money to offset the risk.

It is important to know that Market Makers are important in stocking trading. Taking time to learn and understand what market makers are is a great way to improve your experience when trading stocks. By making use of market makers, you get the chance to find great buy and bid prices quotations that will lead to profits. It is good to know that each market maker always competes for customer order flow by displaying buy and sell quotations for a specific number of shares. Once an order has been received, the market maker instantly sells from its own inventory. This selling process usually takes very little time or seconds.

Chapter 5

What is Regulation S?

Regulation S provides exclusion from Section 5 registration requirements of the Securities Act of 1933 for offerings made outside the United States by U.S and foreign issuers. Securities offering whether public and private made by an issuer outside if the United States in reliance on Regulation S need not to be registered under the Securities Act. It is good to know that Regulation S are non-exclusive, this means that an issuer that attempts to comply with Regulation S may claim availability of another applicable exemption from registration. You need to know that Regulation S is available for offerings for both debt securities and equity.

Regulation S is only available for offers and sales of securities outside the U.S that is made with good intentions and not meant to circumvent the registration provisions of the Securities Act. The availability of the issuer according to Rule 903 and the Resale Rule 904 is contingent if the offer or sale has been made in an offshore transaction and direct selling efforts made by issuer or distributor.

It is important to know that Regulation S is composed of different parts which include eight preliminary notes; Rule 901, which contains a general statement of the regulation; Rule 902, which sets forth applicable definitions; Rules 903 and 904, which set forth the two safe harbors; and Rule 905, which sets forth the resale limitations applicable to equity securities.

Who may rely on Regulation S?

If you are a member of the offering party can rely on Regulation S. Members include U.S issuers, foreign issuers, distributors, affiliates of the issuer, Non U.S. resident purchasers and dealers who are not offering participant as well as U.S. residents who are offering participants.

Who may not rely on Regulation S?

Well, Regulation S is not available for offers and sale securities issued by open end investment companies. Also, investments trust registered or supposed to be registered under the Investment Company Act of 1940 or closed end investment companies required to be registered but not registered under 1940 Act cannot rely on Regulation S.

What types of transactions are conducted under Regulation S?

In the U.S. there are several types of Regulation S that U.S. and foreign issuers many conduct which include:

Standalone Regulation S offering which an issuer carries out an offering of debt in more than one U.S. countries.

A Regulation S offering outside the United States and Rule 144A offering within the U.S

Regulation S offering programs for debt securities that include different types of medium term note programs in the United States under Rule 144A.

You need to know that the other types of offering also allowed by Regulation S include:

-Offerings made under specific conditions pursuant to an employee benefit plan started and administered within the law of the country other than U.S. and also in accordance with the country's practices and documentation.

-Offerings of foreign government securities.

Regulation S part of offering refers to the portion of the offering that requires the offering participants to comply with Regulation S so as to benefit from the safe harbor. It is good to know that offering is also required to comply with the requirements of non U.S. jurisdictions and also requirements of foreign securities exchange or any other listing.

A Regulation S complaint offering can be combined with a registered public offering in the U.S. as well as a structured private or public offering in more than one non U.S. jurisdictions.

What conditions must be satisfied to rely on Regulation S?

It is good to know that the resale safe harbors and issuer of Regulation S can be found in the market participants only if the offer or sale is made as part of an offshore transaction and other directed selling efforts. Also, offerings made in reliance on Rule 903 are seen as additional restrictions that are put in a level of risk that securities in a specific type of transaction follow back.

You need to know that Rule 903 can be explained into three categories of transactions based on the type of securities being offered and sold, whether the issuer is foreign or domestic or the issuer is reporting under the securities Exchange Act of 1934. These categories are as follows.

Category 1: These are transactions in which the securities are less likely to flow back into the United States. So, the only restrictions are that the transaction should be an offshore transaction and that there is no directed selling effort in the U.S.

Category 2 and 3: These are transactions are subject to an increasing number of offering and transactional restrictions for the duration of the applicable known as distribution compliance period. The distribution compliance period is referred to as in Rule 902. This is generally the period following the offering when an offer or sales of category 2 or 3 securities needs to comply with the requirements of Regulation S in order to avoid the flow back of offered securities into the United States. The period usually ranges from 40 days to 6 months for reporting issuers and 1year for equity securities of non-reporting issuers.

Can issuers exempt or excluded offerings concurrently with Regulation S transactions?

Of course. So as to determine if a Rule 903 general requirement for offshore transactions is achieved, a registered offering in the United States will not integrated with the offshore offering that complies with Regulation S. This is because Regulation S indicates that a private placement in the United States may be made in line with an offshore public offering in reliance on the issuer safe harbor. In turn, offshore offerings and sales of securities made in line on Regulation S do not preclude the resale of the exact securities made in reliance on Rule 144A even if the resale takes place during the distribution compliance period.

What are the holding periods applicable to the sale of Regulation S securities?

You need to know that securities cannot be offered or sold to a United States person during the time the distribution compliance period not unless the transaction is registered under the Securities Act. It is important to know that there is no distribution compliance period between securities sold in Category I transaction.

What types of transactions are eligible for exclusion under Regulation S?

Category 1 Transactions

-Category 1 transactions include offerings of:

Securities by foreign issuers who believe at the starting of the offering that there is no SUSMI in some securities, Securities offered by foreign issuer in case of non-convertible debt securities, Securities backed by faith and credit of a foreign government and Securities offered by foreign issuers to an employee benefit plan formed under foreign law.

Category 2 Transactions

-Category 2 transactions include offering of:

Equity securities of reporting foreign issuer, debt securities of a reporting foreign or U.S. issuer and debt securities of a non-reporting foreign issuer.

Category 2 safe harbor is usually available even in cases where there is enough U.S. market interest in the securities. Category 2 securities have a 40 days distribution compliance period.

Category 3 Transactions

-Category 2 transactions include offering of:

Debt offerings by non-reporting Unites States issuers, equity offerings by U.S. reporting issuers and equity offerings by non-reporting issuers

You need to know that Category 3 is a safe harbor due to the fact that it welcomes all transactions that are not eligible for Category 1 or Category 2 safe harbors.

Chapter 5 (Section a)

What is EDGAR?

EDGAR stands for Electronic Data Gathering Analysis and Retrieval System. EDGAR is responsible for performing automated collection, validation, indexing acceptance and forwarding submissions by companies who are expected by the law to file forms with the U.S.A Securities and Exchange Commission (SEC). The main purpose of EDGAR is to ensure there is increase in efficiency and security in the trading market for investors, companies, firms and corporations. The economy is also protected by emphasizing on dissemination, acceptance or receipts and analyzing company's information listed with the agency. It is important to know that public domestic companies are required to carry out their fillings on EDGAR aside for fillings made in paper. Third party fillings such as tender offers or Schedules 13D are also filed on EDGAR.

It is good to note that some documents do not have the permissions to be filed electronically thus they are not available on EDGAR. However, some documents can be filed on EDGAR voluntarily and they can be found or not found on Edgar. Some these documents include Form 144, Forms 3, 4, and 5(these are security ownership and transaction reports filled by corporate insider) as well as filings made by foreign companies or governments.

When it comes to using EDGAR, you need to learn how to use it properly. One of the ways to search EDGAR is by ticker symbol. Although this will give you information, it will not produce all the available tickers. The EDGAR company search page always gives a number of how many companies that can be searched by ticker symbol. It is important to know that you can be able to search for SEC registrants of a certain state by using EDGAR company search. If you want to search for SEC registrants from a particular country, you should simply use the EDGAR company search. However, you need to use the right and current country codes. This is because some countries may have changed their country codes. Finally, you can also use EDGAR company search to find companies of particular industry. It is also good to know that people also can use EDGAR to search for company's former names.

It is important to know that EDGAR has made it possible for information about companies and firms to be distributed online the right way. With the help of EDGAR, individual, Government, firms, Corporation and Companies have been able to find credible information about the specific company they are looking for. The internet has also contributed greatly in making EDGAR to operate well as it does. You need to know that without internet presence, you will not be able to use EDGAR to search for any information.

It is also good to know that EDGAR has helped in improving how businesses and firms operate, thus making it easy and fast to work with companies. With the tight security provides by

EDGAR, firm and company feel safer to maximize their operation and offer more services. You need to know that since the introduction of EDGAR, the mode of operating business and accessing firms information has greatly improved and looking brighter in the future.

Chapter 5 (Section b)

What is the Spread?

In stock trading, you will always come across the term "spread". What is the Spread? This is the difference between the bid and offer price of a security. The spread can also be described as a position established by purchasing one option and selling another option of the same status but of a different series. The spread of a security/asset is usually influenced by different factors. One of the main factors is supply or float. Float is the number of shares outstanding that is available to trade. Other factors are interest in a stock and total trading of the stock. In stock, the spread is the difference between the strike price and the market value.

It is important to know that the spread does not have any hidden cost in trading contrary to what people think. When it comes to trading stocks, your broker doesn't need to make the spread because it is on the other side of the trade. What you need to realize in the stock market, you are rarely trading against your broker. Most of the time, brokers are usually pass through agents. What happens is that your order goes into the market and is matched against what is available. The available trader can be a market maker, institution or even other individual trader. Bottom line, your broker is not allowed to keep that money as profit. The people who greatly profit from spread are market makers who seek to buy at the bid and sell at the offer. They are usually paid for providing liquidity.

Many people are usually misinformed on the term pay in spread. The term "pay" is described as the impact of the spread on your account and importantly you pay half up front and half when you close out the trade. Well, this is not true. It is good to know that you can never "pay" the spread. Incase if you go in and purchase using a market order your trade value will instantly be lower because you will have purchased at the ask price and you will be forced to sell at the lowest bid price. Literally, this money does not come out of your account but as a commission. This is also known as a paper loss.

As a trader, you also need to know that it's not true that the long-term investing is better than short-term trading. For instance, is the spread is $0.50 then it will take a $0.50 move in the market in your favor to overcome that cost. At this point, your holding period doesn't matter. If you trade regularly and following small profits, the spread represent a bigger portion of your gains as well as your commission.

When it comes to spread, there are different types of spread, small spread and large spread. In Small spread, the bid and ask price are very similar to each other. In other words, the spread is a small spread. In the stock market, the small spread occurs when the market is active and has a high number of contracts being traded. In many day trading markets, this happens throughout the trading day, but in other markets, this happens at certain days such as US open.

In large spread, the bid and ask price are very different. The spread is basically a large spread. For instance, if the bid and ask price on the Euro to US Dollar market is at 1.340 and 1.3410 the spread will be 5 ticks. A large spread usually takes place when the market is not actively traded and has a low volume of contracts being traded. For instance, many day trading markets that have small spreads have large spread when waiting for an economic news release or during lunch.

Both small and large spread usually affects the stock market. A small spread is a type of spread that many traders choose since it allows their orders to be filled at the prices they want. Due to this, many day traders temporarily stop trading if their market has a large spread. On the other hand, a large spread causes market orders to be filled at unwanted prices. This requires advance adjustments to the trading system to compensate.

When it comes to trading the spread, some day traders go for trades that take advantage of the spread and in turn these traders prefer a large spread. The trading systems that trade the spread are known as scalping trading systems. The traders are called the scalpers because they want few ticks profit with each trade. A tick is a move that takes place in financial market in different size price increments and the minimum price movement.

Spread betting is also common in the spread. Spread betting is a type of gambling that is used as an alternative to common trading. Spread bets can be placed on different but same markets as regular trading. It is good to know that spread betting is very similar to binary betting but not fixed betting. The spread betting profit and loss also vary with regular trading.

Spread trading is very profitable and a great way to trade. Many traders usually prefer spread trading since it is not possible to use stops in a spread trade. The spread are also considered to lessen the risk in trading. Spreads also require lower margins than any other form of trading, even much lower than the margin requirements for option trading. Another thing is that spread trades are less volatile than any other forms of trading. Due to low volatility the margins for spreads are low. Spread trading is a great way to create a more level playing field because there are no stops. Spread trading is a pure form of trading.

When it comes to spreads, you can take the advantage of inverted markets. When a market is inverted, you have a high possibility of taking profits when the prices are invert and when they return to normal progression.

Chapter 5 (Section c)

What is Going Long vs. Going Short?

In market, we always wonder what investors mean when they talk about going long vs. Going short. Going long vs. Going short are phrases used in financial trading to describe whether a trade was entered by buying or selling. Going long is when a trader is in long trade. This means that they have entered a trade of buying a group of shares and hoping that the prices will go up. A lot of the time, day traders often use the term buy and long interchangeably. Also, some software used in trading have a trade entry button marked as' buy' where other have a trade button marked 'long'. The phrase long is often used to explain a vacant position, this indicate that a trader has an active trade where they purchased a contract in the future market.

Going short is when a trader is in a short trade has gotten into a trade by selling shares and hoping that the price will come down. Just as going long, day traders often us the term sell and short interchangeably. The trading software all trade entry buttons marked 'sell' where another is marked 'short'. The phrase short is used to describe an open position which shows that a trader has an active trade in the future market.

When an investor invests money in stocks, many other investors go long. Meaning they plunk down their money, purchase stocks and hold them in the hope that the stock prices will rise in the future so they can make profits. In other words, they are hoping to buy low and sell high. However, there are other investors that look for stocks they trust are heading down in price for a short term basis. Maybe they believe the company is having financial problems and will handle the situation, or hope the competitors will introduce better products that will affect the company's earnings. Some investors may feel the stock is overly priced and investors have bid up the price of the stock to high level from which stocks are expected to fall. To get profits from what they believe is the stock, these investors go short a process which is also known as selling short.

Investors also borrow shares of the stock from their broker, sell the shares at the current market price and hope to make profits by replacing their borrowed shares with shares that they purchase on the market after the price of stock has dropped. It is important to know that short selling is termed as a risky business. In short selling, brokerage firms let the investor put cash equal to as little as half the value of the securities you are selling short. The investor will also need to pay the interest since the broker will be lending the difference amount you put up initially and the amount of the short sale. If the stock rises in value, borrowing works against you and magnifies your negative rate of return.

As an investor you need to know that your brokerage firm doesn't have to let you go through losses beyond your original investment unless you agree to put up more money. If the value of shares you have invested in rose in a certain point, you will receive a maintenance call from your broker asking you to put more cash or security in your account to cover the growing loss. If you fail to do this, the broker will cover the short and close your position and you would be stuck with any resulting loss. In other words, it is possible to make money whether the stocks rise or fall in value. However, you need to know that selling short is riskier because there is more of a timing element involved.

If an investor decides to buy stock outright, that is ling, it goes down in value. The investor can decide to wait without investing more money. It is good to know that the loss potential is much greater in going short than going long. This also means that to make money by shorting, as an investor you not only have to get the directions of the stock right but you have to be right about pretty short time period. It is important for investors to choose going long and leave short selling to investors who are really good at their game, as in the pros.

When it comes to shorting or selling before buying, many financial markets allow shorting. This is the process of getting into trade by selling and exiting the trade by buying. Selling short or shorting gives professional traders the opportunity to make profit whether the market is moving up or down. This why professional traders only care that the market is moving not keen on which the direction the market is moving.

Chapter Five (Section d)

What is a Bid Price?

We all invest in the stock market for the purpose of growing our investment. Investing in stocks is known to be highly lucrative but at the same time volatile because of fluctuating market prices occasioned by frequent changes in the trading environment. It is important to note that when you choose to invest in stocks, you should have a pretty good idea of how the markets operate and factors that investors in the business should watch out for.

There are different terminologies used in stock markets that you as an investor need to understand. Plying your trade wisely means you need to learn how to grow your investment by using professional stock brokers with a vast understanding of stock trading practices. One of the most crucial terms used in this business is Bid Price. You can never conquer this business unless you understand the implications of how much you are willing to pay to acquire securities on the exchange.

Bid price is the amount an investor is willing to put in to buy a stock. Just as the name suggests, an investor announces the price they are comfortable paying to acquire new stocks. Bid price is basically divided into 2 parts; first, is the price an investor is ready to pay and secondly, the amount of shares one intends to acquire with the quoted bid price. As an investor, you need to discuss with your stock broker and carefully consider your bid price. Smart investing dictates that you should acquire several stocks with a lower bid price to maximize on the profit margins. Bid price is the opposite of ask price which a seller asks for in exchange for selling their shares.

When placing either the bid or ask price, you should remember that both of them are fundamentals in the stock market business. When specifying the bid price, you give an exact amount of how much you are willing to spend on a stock purchase transaction. However, it's essential to point out that the price currently on the market might not be the same price shares last traded hands. This means that investors who want to clearly understand how much they might be required to part with to purchase shares need to know that current market prices don't necessarily mean that's what you will pay for. Bid and ask prices usually differ from current market price indications.

Best Bid is a term used on the stock markets that is important for investors to understand. The definition is similar to bid price with the only difference being best bid referring to highest quoted bid reflecting the highest amount of money an investor is willing to remove to acquire shares. Best bids provide the best price as well as quantity that an investor can acquire from a stock purchase. Best bid is the direct opposite of best Ask.

Best Bid

The National Best Bid and Offer (NBBO) subscribes to SEC requirements to show bid and ask prices that are seen by traders and investors. The SEC advocates for the best prices that customers can access and benefit from. All players in the industry including active traders, short-term traders and day traders refer to the guidelines specified in order to make trading provisions. The NBBO usually ensures that price changes and any other crucial information is frequently updated and customers to gain access to this information.

As an investor, knowing these terminologies is extremely crucial as it enables you to be fully aware of what is expected of you as well how the markets react to various factors. If you have no idea about how to place the best bids, it's often wise to talk to your stock broker.

Chapter Five (Section e)

What is a Short Term Stocks Trade?

There are different types of stocks that you can purchase for your investment. It is important to note that investing in the stock market industry can either be long term, medium or short term. It all depends on what you are intending to achieve and how long you want to be in the business. Short Term Stocks Trade as the name refers is where investors put their money into the stock market for a limited period of time with a certain objectives. Quite a number of investors have become millionaires from short term trading, however, as lucrative as it seems on the surface, it comes with a lot of risks. Periods of trading in a short term stock trade transaction vary, it can either span a few minutes or last up to several days.

The main factor to note here is that this stock trade is considered very lucrative but at the same time comes with a lot of risks. Therefore, if you are intending to become part of this business, having a prior understanding of the risks you are exposing yourself to is critical. The strategies for short term stocks trade are quite different from what would be long term stock investments. A keen eye for detail and thorough understanding of the prevailing market trends as well as events is the best way to ensure success with short term stocks trade. As an investor, you have to learn how to quickly identify good opportunities as well as accurately predict events that are likely to influence the market in certain ways.

With a little research and acquisition of smart trading skills, investors in short term stocks trade can enjoy huge profits from their investments within a short period of time. Understanding the basic concepts and fundamentals of short term trading is the key for successful trading particularly with short term stock transactions. Remember, you are not here for a long time and therefore you must find ways of enabling you to attain your goals in the shortest time possible. The tactics you decide to employ could determine the difference between a profitable venture and a transaction that leads to losses. Keep in mind that how you play your game really matters and determines the level of stake in the investment.

Short term stock investments are about making the right decisions. You should know that there can be no room for mistakes since you have no time to fix blunders. This ideally means that you must distinguish between a good investment and one you have doubts about. Remember, if you are not comfortable about a venture, its better not to risk your money. As a smart investor, you must take time and study the markets before making any moves. This is because short term stock trading counters react very fast and therefore you might not have adequate time to think about the implications of your decisions, everything happens so fast here. A stock that was initially performing well in the earlier hours of the day could take a drastic turn by the time evening closes in. the trick here is that you must know how to engage in the right trade transactions at the right time.

So, how can you achieve this?

- Keep an eye on the moving averages: In case you don't know what moving averages are, this is the average stock price in a specified time period. Here, time frames vary in terms of the number of days. They could be anything from 5 days to as high as 200 days. This is a very important parameter to monitor as it gives you an idea of the stock trend. This way, you can easily determine how a stock is performing and if it is drifting upwards or downwards. A good stock should have a moving average that is constantly on an upward trend as this is an indication that the stock is responding well to the market. Some investors fail to make profits with short term stocks trade because they fail to effectively monitor moving averages and therefore totally lose control of the stock trends. This is quite dangerous as you might never realize when things are going wrong.

- Have knowledge of stock patterns and cycles: It is good to note that stock trades operate in cycles and it's your responsibility to research and have this information at your fingertips before investing. For example, certain months of the year are known to be the best for buying stocks because the prices are low. On the other hand, certain periods such as end year are associated with stock market highs giving investors the best chance to sell their stocks at a high price and make substantial gains on their investment. Understanding these trading cycles is critical as it enables you to ascertain when it is the best time to buy stocks and the ideal time to dispose off your stocks.

- Understand Current Market Trends: This is very important particularly for an investor who wants to gain maximum profits from their investment. Understanding the difference between a negative trend and positive trend holds the key to your success. For instance, if you realize the stocks are reacting negatively to the current market trends, you should avoid buying any more stocks at the time. Also, you might consider shorting just to safeguard your investment in case anything drastic happens. On the other hand, positive trends should encourage you to purchase more stocks and do limited shorting. Bear in mind that when the market trends are not working in your favor, the chances of making any gains from the stock transactions dwindle.

As earlier mentioned, short term stock trade is associated with a lot of risks. One of the key strategies of ensuring success with stock trading is learning how to control risks. Now that you know short term trading is very volatile and risky, you have to come up with ways of reducing risk and maximize returns. It's painful to see your hard earned investment go down the drain and therefore it imperative to minimize risk as much as possible. One good way of reducing and controlling risk is to use buy stops and sell stops as a protection strategy.

A Sell Stop is whereby you order your stock to be sold the moment it attains a certain predetermined monetary value. When this price is attained, the stock must be sold at the current market price. A Buy Stop on the other hand is an instruction to purchase a stock when it rises and qualifies as a buy order. These simple strategies have helped stock investors to remain safe and effectively control their risks. In typical cases, short term trading principles advise that you should set your buy stop and sell stop within a 15% margin of the initial value you used to acquire the stocks or initiated the stock. The main reason for doing this is to prevent huge losses and instead focus on acquiring more gains on your investment.

Having thorough knowledge of what affects the stock is critical for those who want to succeed in the stock market. There are several factors that affect the market and dictate stock prices. Issues such as pricing and earnings have dictate strongly how the markets will react and therefore you should be prepared to be stay ahead of everyone else. Technical analysis enables you to have a clear understanding of the inside happenings that affect the stock market industry. As an investor, knowledge of technical analysis is critical particularly when it comes to understanding previous stock trends and predicting what will happen in the future.

Technical aspects involve issues such as understanding of patterns which is instrumental in achieving good results. You should know that patterns change in depending on what is happening on the market. Investors who succeed in the stock market have mastered the science behind patterns and how to use this information to analyze and predict price changes.

You can use several techniques to make money with short-term stocks. In order to be successful, you need to know how to use various tools and technical skills available to effectively study market trends and maximize on your investment. When this information is used properly, you can be able to make substantial financial gains from an industry that is considered to be quite volatile.

Many investors who opt for short Term Stocks Trade are in the business to maximize their investments within a short period of time. It is therefore important to equip yourself with information that is based on unique strategy and methodologies of conquering market patterns with an aim of making profits. When trading in short term stocks, your main aim is to trade wisely and make as much profit as possible within the shortest period of time. You should know that this type of trading is quite lucrative but also has its own risks.

Getting enough information and understanding the key concepts of smart trading is the key to success.

Chapter 5 (Section f)

What is a Micro-Cap Stock?

Investors interested in the stock market industry have a variety of investment ventures to choose from. When venturing into the stock exchange market, it is always important to have a thorough understanding of the various types of stocks available in order to make an informed decision and make a selection of an investment that lies within your budgetary provisions.

A Micro-Cap stock is traded in public companies in the United States whose market capitalization base lies between $50 million and $ 300 million. Therefore, if you choose to buy shares from public U.S. companies that fall within the described market capitalization value, ideally, you have invested in Micro-cap stocks. It is important however to differentiate between micro-cap stocks and nano stocks as some investors tend to confuse the 2. Companies with a market capitalization of less than $50 million fundamentally deal with nano stocks. An important distinction to keep in mind is that companies dealing with nano caps have a smaller market capitalization base as compared to micro-cap companies. However, small, medium and large and mega cap corporations carry a greater market capitalization value.

It's interesting to note that companies with a higher market capitalization don't necessarily have stocks that carry a higher price tag as compared to their counterparts with smaller market capitalizations. A key secret that every investor should know is that the main critical factor to watch out for here is stability. Investing in firms with a larger market capitalization means fewer risks for the investor. However, the pitfall here is the level of risk dictates how lucrative the returns would be. This means that if you invest in a company with a small market capitalization, the stock is more risky but then your chances of achieving good returns are substantially increased.

Micro cap stocks have the potential to attract a lot of returns but investors have to be very careful because their risky nature can lead to serious catastrophes. Potential investors need to know that this is a risky venture that could have either outcome. Researching on the internet and gathering enough information and facts about Micro cap stocks is essential before making financial commitments.

A question that many people ask is 'what is market capitalization and how do you know the market capitalization value of a company?   The answer is simple, Market Capitalization measures the value of outstanding shares of a company. The value is then obtained by multiplying the stock price with the sum number of outstanding shares of a company.

There are many companies out there dealing with Micro-Cap stocks. It is your responsibility as an investor to research thoroughly and select an investment venture that you feel will help you to quickly attain your financial goals. Understanding what micro-cap stocks are is a key requirement for any potential investor. There is a lot of information that you can be able to find on the internet to enable you have a deeper understanding of micro-cap stocks and how to become a successful trader.

Chapter Six

What is Day Trading?

Day trading is described as the buying and selling of security within one day of trading. This can take place in any marketplace but it's mostly common in stock market and foreign exchange market. It is good to know that day traders usually invest a lot of many and they are well educated. Day traders use huge amounts of leverage and shorter trading plans to make use of small price movements in highly liquid stocks. You need to know that day traders serve two main important functions in the market place which includes: making sure the market runs effectively and providing market liquidity in stock market.

When it comes to day trading, there are a lot of controversies. When you search online, you will come across a lot of debates on profits gained in day trading. Many internet scams usually take advantage of these controversy and scam traders. Unfortunately, media continues to promote this trading as a get rich quick scheme that works. Those people who decide to engage in this trading without carrying out enough research first lose a lot of money. On the other hand there are traders who get successful in day trading.

A lot of professionals and financial experts advise people not to shy away from day trading. A lot of traders who engage in day trading wisely have reported huge profits. Experts report that there is a lot of money in day trading, the key thing is to trade wisely so as to be successful. However, before you engage in day trading, it is important to understand the risk and complexity involved. Moreover, the need to understand how the markets operate and strategies to use so as to make short term profits is essential.

What makes a good day trader?

A good day trader has the knowledge and experience needed in the market. A person who want to get into day trade without understanding the market important factors often end up losing a lot of money. There is a lot of information on the internet that you can use to become a better day trader.

Before you venture into day trading, you need to have enough capital. It is good to know that many day traders don't expect to make money day trading. Most day traders use risk capital which they can comfortably afford to lose. This not only protects them from financial ruin but it also helps them get rid of emotions while trading. In most cases, a huge amount of capital is used to capitalize effectively on the day price movements.

Having a strategy as a day trader is also very important. As a trader you need to be an edge higher than the rest of the market. There are different strategies that day traders use such as arbitrage, swing trading and trading news to mention but a few. Most of these strategies are improved until they produce great profits and limit losses.

As a day trader you need to have discipline. To have a great strategy in day trading, you need to have discipline. Many day traders end up losing a lot of money because they fail to deal with trades that meet their own criteria. Having a plan to trade and trading with a plan is very important if you want to succeed in day treading.

If you plan to get into day trading for a living it is essential to know that there are two primary divisions of professional day traders. There are those who work alone and others who work as an institution. Many day traders who trade for a living work as a big institution. These traders have access to many things such as large amounts of capital and leverage, expensive analytical software and a direct line to a dealing desk that individual traders cannot get. Traders who work as an institution always look for easy profits that can be made from arbitrage opportunities and news events. The ability to access resources allows them to focus on less risky day trades prior individual traders can react.

It is good to know that many individual traders manage other people's money or trade with their own money. Individual traders have no access to dealing desk but they have strong ties to a brokerage and access to resources. This is due to the large amounts of commission spending. However, some of these resources prevent individual traders from competing directly with institution day traders thus forced to take more risks. As an individual trader, you should be ready to day trade using technical analysis and change trades combined with some leverage. This will enable you to generate enough profits on small price movements in highly liquidity.

What Does A Day Trader Require?

When it comes to day trading, it demands access to some complex financial services and tools in the marketplace. Being a day trader you need the access to the trading desk. The trading desk is usually meant for traders working with larger institutions or traders who deal with large amounts of money. The trading desk gives these traders with adequate order executions which is important especially when high price movement takes place. For instance, when an acquisition is named, day traders looking at merger arbitrage get their orders in before the rest of the market thus taking advantage of the price difference.

A day trader also requires multiple news sources. It is good to have important information on commodity when trading. You need to know that news provide many opportunities to day traders to focus on, so it's important to be the first to know when something major happens. A common trading room contains access to the Dow Jones Newswire, televisions showing CNBC and other news agencies, as well as software that analyze different news sources for important stories.

Having access to trading software is also important for day traders. Those traders who depend on technical indicators or exchange trades rely more on the software than news. This software simply contains features such as automatic pattern recognition, Broker integration, Genetic and neural applications and back testing. By combining these tools a trader get a way ahead over the rest of the marketplace. Inexperienced traders who decide not to use these tools end up losing a lot of money.

It is good to know that although day trading can have some risks its can make one money if carried out the right way. Day traders, both individual and institutional play a major role in the marketplace by keeping the market liquid and efficient. Some people many argue that individuals should avoid from day trading while others suggest that it's a good way to make profit. Although day trading is become very popular today among inexperienced traders, it should be left for those with enough knowledge, experience and skills in day trading.

Those people who get into day trading always want to make a lot of money with minimal effort. Traders who get into day trading with this mentality always lose money. However, using a good strategy that you are comfortable trading with, you can improve your chances of succeeding in day trading. When it comes to evaluating performance, many day traders evaluate performance based on percentage of gain or loss. Knowing the right strategies of day trading is a good way to identify common day trading problems and know how to solve them.

If you are planning to day trade, you need to know that day trading is challenging to master. As a result, many people who try it flop. However, this should not discourage anyone who wants to get into day trading. All you need to do is to take your time and learn how to succeed in day trading. Using the right strategy, practicing and evaluating your performance consistently is a great way to improve your chances of becoming a pro in day trading.

Chapter Six (Section a)

Why Day Trade Penny Stocks?

Day trading is a great way to make profits on the penny stocks market. It is good to know that it is not challenging to start day trading penny stocks and be able to make a profit as soon as you start. Traders have been able to make profits on penny stocks on a day by day basis. Day trading penny stocks requires one to follow many stocks. Most of these stocks will not make any important moves for day to day. Most of the times, penny stocks will have plenty of activity and volatility on a day to day basis but they can always drop overnight.

Many investors have become successful in day trading penny stocks. You need to know that high liquidity penny stocks can enable day traders to move in and out for a profit. Within a few minutes or hours, a successful day trader can make hundreds of dollars trading penny stocks. If you are still wondering what is day trading, well day trading is the process of buying a selling a stock within the same day for a small price movement. Some day traders usually buy and sell in a few seconds while others wait for few minutes or even hours to finally find a price movement that allows good profits.

Penny stocks with liquidity can be volatile and increase in price a lot of times throughout the trading day. One of the huge advantages of day trading penny stocks rather than keeping them overnight is that you never know what will happen after the market closes. A company could announce a negative press release that can make the stock to go down and suffer huge losses.

If you are planning on engaging in day trading penny stocks, you need to find a great service that offers level trading quotes in real time. Having information of what price a penny stock is trading at each moment is very important. Also being aware what is the best bud and ask quotes associates with stock orders is also essential. Being knowledgeable of what investors are bidding or selling plays a critical part to achieve your success in penny day stock trading. Knowing all these information will guide you to determine the position you want your stock and when you want to buy or sell.

As a trader, you should never get into day trading not unless you are able to effectively monitor the holdings and be dedicated to proper mind set. The penny stock world is very simple to understand. All you need to know is that penny stocks do not cost a lot of money and they bring huge profits quickly when trading them.

Before you get into penny stock trading, you need to check the prices of stocks. Having a computer and internet connectivity to your broker is necessary. When day trading penny stocks, you may need to check the stock prices frequently and watch the stock prices all day. Using a computer it will take a few minutes of your time and you will be able to get the prices, submit new orders and alter orders online as well as check penny stock activity.

As an investor in penny stock day trading, you need to have patience. Although day trading in penny stocks is one of the quickest profit and loss methods in the financial world, you need to have patience. The best penny stock day trading method involve going for a week or so without trading since you have to wait to get the best prices. You need to know that being impatient gets in the way of effective day trading strategy. Getting involved in day trading penny stocks has a lot of advantages.

One of the main benefits why you need to day trade penny stocks is the fact that you have high chances of avoiding scams. It is important to know that penny stocks are very risky and a common ground for scammers. Am sure you have heard stories of investors losing a lot of money in penny stock trading. You need to know that there are few penny stocks scams that are out there. By day trading penny stocks, you are able to use your money and make profits fast. Day trading penny stocks does not allow you to keep your money long term hence scammers don't get the chances of spending your investment. No one wants to lose their money to fraudster and scammer. Taking advantage of trading your penny stocks within the day is a great way to prevent yourself from getting scammed.

By engaging in day trading penny stocks you are also able to maximize on profit particularly if the shares go up. In stock trading, the prices keep changing every time. As a trader, it is important to keep checking the prices of the stocks every time. Failing to check how the prices are faring can cost you huge profits. By keeping tight watch of penny stock trading will enable you to sell or buy shares when the prices are great for you to make the profits. In penny stock trading, you never know what will happen tomorrow, prices may be good today and awful tomorrow. This is the reason why as a penny stock trader, you need to take advantage of day trading and make sure maximize on the profits.

Deciding to day trade penny stocks is also a good way to raise capital for an investment. If you have an investment at your hands and have part of the money, you can easily raise the other part by stock trading. Experienced and skilled stock traders usually raise a lot of money through day penny stock trading. Once they know how shares are faring and know when the prices are doing well, they capitalize on the great prices and raise capital for their investments.

By day trading penny stocks, you have the right to try different shares from different companies. This is a great way to make money through penny stocks. It is good to know that penny stocks usually have different profit margins depending on the company. In case you trade penny stocks of a certain company today, you can go ahead and trade different penny stocks of another company the following day if they have great profits. This way, many traders have been able to avoid losses and concentrate on penny stocks of specific companies that guarantee profits daily. Penny stock traders with knowledge and skills in stock trading have ended up making a lot of money through this process since they capitalize on companies that have shares with prices going up.

Choosing to day trade penny stocks also enables investors to monitor and analyze stock trading better. When one decided to trade multiple stocks, following and monitoring each stock can be overwhelming. However, by choosing specific penny stock to trade for the day enables one to keep track of the prices hence monitoring and analysis becomes simpler. This way, one can effectively predict when low stock is moving. Once high stock is on motion, one can sell their penny stocks and make profit for that day without risking their investment.

Chapter Six (Section b)

How Do You Make Money in Day Trading?

Today, there is a lot of information indicating that day trading is dangerous and unprofitable. This is not true because many people have been able to make a lot of money through day trading. Day trading involves people buying and selling stocks quickly during the course of the day. When day traders want to make money, they often pursue companies with high businesses that are more aggressive than the overall marketplace. The most aggressive stocks in the marketplace are often penny stocks which trade for less than $5. Day traders prefer quick gains since they hope to make profits within a short while.

It is important to know that the financial system is very complex than it used to be years back. The reason why stock market continues to trade is because companies require money to grow. When a company reaches a certain point, they need more money so as to expand. A private company turns public and that is when it appears in the stock market. With time, the company grows even bigger and they stop lending money from friends, family and local banks. In turn, they go public so as to receive money they need to keep growing and compete in their industry. Once you invest in a company via stock market, you literally become a part owner of the company.

You need to know that there millions of shares of stock for certain companies. Each company is usually placed in a group of stocks known as indexes. Platforms such as NASDAQ comprise index commonly known for consisting technology stocks. When a company goes public people start investing in it. The left shares have value and the general public decides what value is based on the stock market. This is the reason why stock market exists and the main ways that experienced day traders use to make real money in stock market. To explain further, day traders buy and sell stocks based on their future value.

<u>Where is the money in day trading?</u>

Getting into day trading, you need to be careful so as not to lose money. Traders who start day trading without doing proper research on day trading have 80% chances of failing at day trading. If you are new to day trading, taking it slow to learn how the trade operates is a great way to make money at the end. Deciding to run a brokerage that is paid commissions for every sale a day trader makes is a great way to make money in day trading. Even at a cost of $1 per trade, 30 trades per day for 200 days per year will amount to around $6000. To increase your profits, enable day traders borrow from you on a margin. This way, you will make more than $2000 yearly in interest payment on every $$25,000 they borrow.

People who benefit from day trading are those that don't actually day trade. You have high chances of getting profits by taking your time, researching and looking for legit and organized companies with real competitive deals. Although you may not get rich quick, you have a high chance of making enough money.

When it comes to day trading, there are different ways that you can make money day trading. Day trading for someone else is great way to earn money. To venture into this, you need to complete an in house training program for the firm you represent. For investment houses, you will get a decent base salary between about 50,000 – 70,000 dollars US enough to keep you at a lower middle class city such as New York. Although this is not enough to take care of needs such as vacations, car, dinners or private schools among other, this means that you have to work extra hard to make your bonus. The only catch is you have to make money day trading. The advantage of trading with a company is over time the amount of money you can use will increase and you face no downside risk since it's the company's money. The important thing is to make sure you have enough money under management. On average, an experiences day trader in New York trading for a company makes between 250k and 500k day trading if they are above average. A middle trader can expect between 100k and 175k. Other benefits that comes with day trading for a company include health benefits, no risk of personal capital, prestige of working for an investment bank and high chances of moving up the cooperate ranks to manage various funds.

Day trading for a prop firm is also a great way to earn money in day trading. Day trading for prop firms can at time be challenging. Just like to trading for company, you will get some training before the prop firms gives you the go ahead to trade with their money and have access to their systems. You need to know that trading for a prop firm and company differ greatly. You should not expect any health care of paid time off and you will not have a base salary or annual reviews. As a trader, the prop firm will require to deposit some money so as to start using them. The advantage of dealing with prop firms is the fact that they generally split profits with you anywhere from a 3% upwards to 50%. The disadvantage is not having a salary and you feel the most pain when losses occur. On normal day, an above average trader for a prop firm makes around 150k to 250k a year. An average trader makes between 60k and 100k.

Day trading for yourself is also a great way of making money in day trading. As a trader, you inner part may only want to see limitless possibilities. When day trading for yourself you should not first think of making millions. You need to have realistic objectives and figures. First of all, day trading is difficult more than a sales job or entrepreneurship when it comes to steady income. The outcome can be at times unbearable if you don't manage a steady paycheck. You need to know that in day trading a lot of effort does not mean greater results. Your earning potential is in equivalent to the initial capital you invested and monthly expenses. Instead of mentioning how much money you can make day trading for yourself , you need to give yourself a range of how much you can earn based on the capital you invested prior trading. Day trading for yourself can be stated with capital less than $50k. If you are planning to day trade with less than $50kand you have monthly expenses, you will run out of money within 6 – 24 months. It is important to know that the SEC requires one to have a minimum of 25k to start day trading.

What you need to know is that day trading has money but you need to approach the venture in the right way. Taking time to research on the right way that suits you to make money day trading, you will be able to choose the right method and in turn make money in day trading. Asking for help on how to make money in day trading from day trading experts is also a great way to maximize your options before engaging in day trading.

Chapter Six (Section c)

Isn't Day Trading Risky

We all have our investment and trading habits that we feel will yield the most benefit from our investments. The stock market has in the recent past become one of the most popular investment platforms for the modern day investor. When you choose to do stocks, ideally, you should have made up your mind whether you want to be in for the short term or long term. Day trading is a concept that is quickly picking up momentum particularly for investors who want to exit the markets fairly quickly before unmanageable risks begin to take shape.

Many have said day trading is safe but looking at it critically, it also has its own pitfalls that investors need to be aware of. The trading habits that one adopts can play a huge role in determining the kind of results you are likely to achieve at the end of the day. Day traders prefer to buy and sell their securities within the same day and steer clear of any overnight price movements. Surprisingly, this trade is so common that some people actually make a living from day trading.

To succeed, you must ensure that you are ready to attain either extreme profits or losses since the markets could either sway either way. When you decide to be a day trader, you need to keenly evaluate various securities on the market and choose the stocks that exhibit clear characteristics to trade on positive grounds. Of course, you need to exercise a lot of discipline and stick to your own set of rules that work for you the best. Some traders also have poor money management skills that lead them to executing poor trades that fail to materialize and bring in any substantial profits.

As a trader, you must be prepared to absorb any risks that could come with day trading. The risk capital used should be sufficient enough to safeguard you from any extremes. Some day traders borrow money and use it to trade securities on the market, this means that you must have a framework in place to repay your debts whichever way the trading goes. Insiders who understand the market know that day trading is very lucrative but at the same time comes with numerous risks. Before engaging in this trading, you must research and understand the risks that you expose yourself to particularly when you fail to attain the anticipated profits.

Ideally, experts urge traders to go slow on day trading until the fully comprehend the ropes of the game and how they can maximize their chances of having a breakthrough. When you engage in day trading, you literally put all your stakes at risk and therefore it's imperative to do all you can to ensure that there is no room for mistakes. Ideally, a loss should occur because of other market factors other than your carelessness.

Well, every investment has its own risks and therefore if you decide to engage in day trading. You should ensure that your strategies are well researched and tested to evaluate their suitability and capability to make profits. Day traders gain experience the more they do transactions on the exchange and therefore with time are better placed to understand the challenges that accompany this trade.

When you carry out an analysis, you will realize that a lot of theories and speculations have been associated with day trading. What many traders fail to understand is that your success as a day trader has a lot to do with your personality, money management skills, understanding the risks involved as well as carefully approaching all your trade executions with strategy and caution. Today, there are numerous opportunities that day trading presents for industry players. It is important to therefore consider all the pros and cons of this type of trading before deciding to execute transactions. Fortunate traders have managed to reap a lot of benefits from day trading despite the high levels of risk involved.

If you are contemplating becoming a day trader, you probably need to be educated in detail about the benefits and risks involved with this kind of business. So, if you're torn in between day time trading and other types of trading, you probably need to evaluate things in detail. After going through both the merits and demerits of day trading, it's time to make decision and determine whether you are ready for this style of trading. Remember that day time trading is not for the faint hearted, if you can't live with the risks that are associated with this trade, you're probably better off in another investment venture.

If you are planning in investing in day trading it is important to know both the advantages and disadvantages.

Advantages of day trading
You have your money at the beginning and the end of the day. Unlike other investment plans, day trading allows you to keep your money throughout the day and use it when you want to. If you don't feel like trading on that day, you simply keep your money and wait until the day you feel like trading.

With day trading, you have the ability to trade more opportunities because you can have more than 4 times your account equity buying power within the day.

As an investor you earn interest on your overnight cash balance. One of the main reasons non-traders keep off from using margin is because they have to pay interest when you use it. Many brokers usually leave money in an interest bearing account, so when you have money in it you will literally be making money.

You get statistically meaningful sample size for more quickly. Since you will have a lot of opportunities to trade, you will be able to find larger sample size much more quickly. This is very important for successful trading.

You don't need to pay attention to the news. How prices are faring in the marketplace is always announced in the news. You don't need to worry about holding overnight when a firm is releasing earnings and at what time. You don't need to get worried how to react to news.

Day trading is less risky. This is because you will be avoiding the overnight gaps with proper money management that you can really have better control of your risk.

Disadvantages of Day Trading Stock

Day trading is very time consuming. Most day traders spend their entire day in front of computers. Anyone who considers day trading stock will not be able to work at a day job due to their nature of day trading.

When it comes to day trading options, one should have his or her own broker account. Due to the nature of day trading one will not have adequate time to call a good broker to carry out the trades expeditiously since options can be sometimes be bought and sold within minutes all day long. If you decide to still use a broker, the commissions paid brokers engage in day trading stock are very high that day trading is often unprofitable to the investor.

Day trading risks can also be very costly. Day trading in stock is simply not for people who have knowledge and skills. For traders who don't have enough knowledge and skills when it comes to day trading, it is likely they will make common mistakes thus losing money. Those people who make profit in day trading stock options have a lot of experience thus enabling them to have competency and technical knowledge that is required to make decisions in day trading.

It is also great to know that volatility is given when day trading stocks. The volatility of the market usually changes from time to time during the day. This is one of the reasons why day trading stocks should only be left to be with enough skills and knowledge needed to successfully day trade. Venturing into day trading without proper skills will only harm your investment and you will lose your money.

When it comes to day trading, it can also be quite costly. Until you practice and learn about words and terms used in day trading stocks, making mistakes regularly is expected. This is the reason why one needs to have available capital not only for initial investment s and regulations when day trading stocks but also allows one to avoid mistakes. Thought this seems like a great way to get rich quickly, the disadvantages of day trading stocks should be put in mind.

These are some of the advantages and disadvantages that an investor should be aware of prior deciding to venture into day stock trading.

Chapter Six (Section d)

Why Not Day Trade Blue Chip Stocks?

It is important to know that many investors usually think the best way of making money ion stock trading by investing in long term stocks such as blue chip stocks. Many stock traders usually view blue chip stocks to have the highest value. In the market place the word "blue chip" is referred to high value stocks as determined by their wellbeing, financial strength in good and bad market conditions as well as paying dividends.

Many investors especially new ones usually choose to invest in blue chips instead of trying on smaller firms until they become more experienced in trading stocks. Blue chip stocks are perceived as being more risky than other stocks. A well-established company usually has more resources to draw on a larger brand to keep it higher compared to small startup. This does not mean that Blue Chip Stocks Companies do not suffer from price fluctuations and volatility but this makes them to face less risk.

Other investors choose to invest in blue chip stocks because of their age or portfolio size. People who are nearing retirement usually avoid risking large amount of capital on risky stocks since they do not many years to wait for the prices to go up. Also, those with huge amounts of money choose to invest in blue chips which have more liquidity than other smaller counterparts. Putting a lot of money into smaller stocks can push the prices temporarily up thus giving a poor average dollar cost. Others are better valuing and analyzing bigger firms with long track records than the newer and smaller firms.

Investing in blue chip stocks can be in different ways. One of the methods is to purchase shares of the companies listed in an index. Another way is to buy a managed fund such as Alpha Australia Blue Chip Fund that focuses long term capital growth with steady increasing dividends. Also you can buy an Exchange Traded Fund (ETF) aimed at blue chip stocks. EFT allows intra-day trading compared to traditional managed mutual funds.

Many experts in day trading usually warn investors to stay away from long term day trading. This is due to the fact that day trading does not advocate for long term investing since there are a lot risks involved. It is good to know that a lot of scammers usually prey on penny stocks being invested long term. This is the reason why many traders choose to day trade their penny stocks daily. The fact that blue chips are long term penny stocks; it is not a good idea to invest in them because you may end up losing a lot of money. This does not mean that you should not invest in blue chips stocks. However, you need to know that blue chips are made for long term investment thus making them not favorable for day trading compared to normal penny stocks.

Since blue chips are long term investment that offers many advantages to investors, they also have different disadvantages and risks that need to be considered such as effects of interest rates and inflation, business risk and liquidity. The ability to change an investment into money is called liquidity. Also a liquid investment is one that can be easily changed into cash. On the other hand, an illiquid investment is not easily converted into cash. An investment is said to be marketable if it can be easily sold in the marketplace. The disadvantage of day trading blue chip stocks is the fact that it's illiquid. Other day trading penny stocks may be converted into cash but only with an amount of loss. Long term investments such as blue chips stocks are therefore not ideal for earning income to meet rising responsibility such as medical and living expenses.

It is also important to know that holding onto investments for longer periods also exposes an investor to increased business risks. This is the risk the business you invest in become less profitable hence deteriorating the value of your investment. Long term fixed investment such as blue chips stocks run the risk of their value decreasing sue to rise in interest rates. Also inflation need to be taken into consideration when planning on future returns for long term investments. You need to know that your investment returns must overtake inflation in order to increase your buying power. In general, long term investment such as blue chip stocks offer the potential for higher returns but one need to keep in mind the risks and dangerous as well.

Day trading blue chips stocks can lead to losing an investment. A great way of looking at cash that has divided is to explain it as a payment that can go to general business expansion, talent acquisition or R&D. Unlike other firms that reinvest their profits, dividend distributing companies intentionally lower their financial roots. In these modern times, economic change can affect the firm's financial position and those that pay investors become even more vulnerable during this time.

Trying to day trade blue chip stocks can make the stocks volatile investments. The price of each stock can vary from different from day to day and the factors that cause the price to infatuate at times are beyond the control of an investor. If you are an investor nearing retirement, you stay away from day trading blue chips stocks. This because blue chips stocks are long term and one needs to wait for a long period of time so as to get profit from them. As a retiree you need to keep off such investment because you don't have the time for such investment to make money. It is better you day trade normal penny stocks that you are guaranteed of making profits the same day. Also you don't need to invest in stocks you can no longer afford or take chances on your money. Remember, you are operating on your retirement funds.

Day trading blue chips stocks does not guarantee increased value within the day. This is because they take years to increase in value slowly and mature. For investors who need a high yield in a very short time, day trading long term investments such as blue chip stocks is not the right move. A lot of fees that are associated with these stocks of investments and small fluctuations may be too much for someone who is looking for profits daily.

Bottom line, blue chip stocks are great investment for any investor who is looking for long term profits. If you are thinking of making money by day trading blue chips stock this is not a good idea at all. Remember that the nature of blue chips stocks is meant for long term not daily trading like penny stocks. You only need to trade blue chips stocks if you are not in a hurry to make money in a short time. If you are willing to wait for some few years for the stocks to mature then you can go ahead and trade blue chips stocks. However, if you are looking for fast profits within the day and you are not willing to risk your investment then you should go ahead and day trade penny stocks. Another thing investing in blue chips stocks is more expensive compared to penny stocks. This is the reason there are a lot of opportunities trading penny stocks daily compared to blue chips stocks.

Chapter 7

How Should I Trade My Penny Stocks?

The success of any penny stock investor depends on how smart you are at the game. Remember, when you decide to venture into stock trading, you potentially put your money into a lottery that could swing either way. This means that you have to be very careful and understand the rules of the trade before plunging into the business. Penny stocks are an interesting investment particularly when your decision to invest is backed up by enough market information and solid facts. Everyone has their own approach and tactics of trading penny stocks, the approach you decide to take should constitute a winning strategy that will grow your investment to unprecedented levels of success.

The general public perception is that penny stocks are risky, volatile and unreliable. While some of these perceptions could actually be genuine, the approach you use to carry out your trade carries the day. While it is perfectly fine to research and see how others have managed their penny stocks, you need to choose what is right and beneficial for your trading experience. Quite a number of investors have put in place strategies that have helped them to steadily graduate from penny stocks to medium or large cap stocks.

If you want to become a smart penny stock trader, there are some fundamental rules and practices that need to be part of you. Penny stocks have become quite popular these days but lack of understanding on their trading methodologies can potentially ruin an entire investment. If you want to have a successful investment story, you need to be smart in all dealings and also be above board. It is important to study the market and come up with sustainable investment decisions in order to be considered a successful penny stock investor.

Whenever you decide to become part of penny stock traders, you need to carefully evaluate your financial position. In other words, before putting your money in the stock market, make sure you have enough cash to run your daily activities. Do not make the mistake of treating penny stocks as a lottery since this has caused many investors to lose their entire investments. Whenever you identify penny stocks, you feel are worth investing, be sure to keep aside money that can cater for emergencies in case they occur.

Wise investment dictates that you have to understand the risk of any investment before putting your money into it. When it comes to penny stocks, you should dedicate some of your time and investigate why penny stocks are considered risky. If you are to succeed in this business, you must have an understanding of the challenges and learn how to successfully navigate them once you are in the business. Certain factors are known to responsible for the risks associated with penny stocks. Absence of minimum standards, lack of information, no solid financial history and other factors negatively affect penny stocks and therefore you have to trade wisely to avoid getting affected by risks associated with penny stocks.

It is said penny stocks are not for the fainthearted and therefore it's always a good idea to gradually approach the idea of investing in penny stocks rather than rushing into a venture you don't fully understand. The stock market industry is very complex and having a prior idea of how it operates is a good idea. Before plunging into the murky field of penny stocks, you should first try out mid and large cap stock to have an idea of the industry. Doing this sets a good precedence and gives you prior trading experience that will be of benefit trading penny stocks.

Penny stocks have their own language and terminologies that you need to understand. You need to make use of all facilities at your disposal as well as have a thorough comprehension of issues such as money flow, market capitalization and share structure. Successful penny stock investors understand the need to trade within the trading structures as well as understand what is required of them. Taking time to understand the tactics of trade governing penny stocks is absolutely critical for anyone who wants join the league of successful penny stock investors.

Understanding how to succeed as a penny stock investor means you need to know your limits. Every business has its ugly side that any entrepreneur shouldn't venture. The same fate applies to penny stocks. There are some situations that you need to completely avoid if you want success to come your way when trading penny stocks. In this business, you shouldn't trust anyone especially email messages that you get encouraging you to buy stocks of particular companies. Sometimes, some of these campaigns are stage managed by insiders who simply want to create demand for their penny stocks for their own selfish interests. When you receive such offers, you should be wary and be careful with the decisions you make. Other ventures you shouldn't attempt are choosing to buy stocks with companies you don't like or going for firms with low revenue margins.

If you don't want to be disappointed when trading penny stocks, you should learn to pinpoint red flags and know when it's too risky to engage. Penny stocks have in the past been associated with several scams and stock dilution scandals. When you feel you are trading on dangerous grounds, it's always good to withdraw before it becomes too late.

Penny stocks can be more rewarding if you purchase shares with companies that are on a consistent path of growth. With proper research, it's always possible to pinpoint the companies that are doing well and making profits. Buying penny stocks from such companies could prove to be expensive but a better decision in the long run as your risk levels are substantially reduced. So, when shopping for companies to buy penny stocks, try to establish their financial stability and track record of success. Obviously, it would be good to avoid firms that are struggling with debt and stock prices may face too many fluctuations and uncertainty.

Some investors get into penny stocks viewing them as a lottery game for purposes of enjoyment. Any venture you invest your money into ceases becoming a hobby and become a real business where you have to strive for success. Some people end up losing their investments in penny stocks because they don't treat these stocks with the seriousness they deserve. Trading smartly as a penny stock investor means you have to be ready to spend quality time understanding various trading patterns with an aim of making the right decisions. The only way to succeed in this business is to treat it as a business rather than a mere hobby.

If you are managing an online portfolio, it's always better to keep a balance of the stocks that you decide to invest in. The safest approach to trade in penny stocks is to ensure that you don't allow your investment to exceed 5% value of your entire portfolio. The reason is pretty simple – you want to spread your investment across different stock markets and avoid placing all your eggs into one basket. Over committing an investment into penny stocks is risky as serious losses could occur in case the stocks take a turn for the worse.

Technology has offered sustainable solutions and made it increasingly easier for penny stock investors to track their investments. We are living in the digital era and you cannot afford to downplay the role that technology plays particularly when it comes to accurate and timely monitoring as well as tracking of stock markets. Nowadays, we have investment management software applications that help you to make better investment decisions based on a number of analytic parameters. Use of these tools allows for smart decision making which in turn helps to safeguard your interests in the penny stock business.

If you don't have proper knowledge on how to trade penny stocks, make sure you educate yourself before joining the marketplace. Please bear in mind that there is no room for ignorance in this business. You have to understand the implications of each and every decision you make as well as keep an eye on the counters while skillfully applying the knowledge you have learnt to make sound decisions. The stock market industry is quite vast and there are important fundamentals of trading that you need to grasp in order to compete effectively and grow your investment.

You don't need to become a guru to trade in penny stocks. Understanding simple and core principles such as money management is critical particularly if you want to become a successful penny stock investor. To achieve this, you need to adopt a strong reading and research culture in order to keep up with the new market trends as well as understand the insider perspective of penny stock trading.

Knowing when to quit is absolutely essential as it helps to safeguard your investment particularly in times of trouble. Every investment has its limit and if you feel the markets are heading towards doom, you should never wait for the worst to happen. Experienced investors always know when it is time to withdraw their investment particularly when they realize that all is not well. In this business, you have to be ready to make drastic decisions without a second thought particularly if your investment is under serious jeopardy.

The stock market industry is a collective responsibility and team work from all investors. To become better at the game, you need to allow those who are more experienced than you are to mentor you. Teaching life experiences and learning from those who have been there before you place you in a better position as a penny stock investor. One way to learn and be mentored is joining a trade advisory service where you get a chance to interact with experts. This way, you receive practical hands on skills that any penny stock investor should know.

With all the above considerations in mind, you are assured that your journey as a penny stock investor will be smooth and rewarding. We all have different approaches and styles of penny stock trading, the most important thing is to ensure that you trade within the defined structures and regulations.

Chapter 7 (Section a)

What is Payment for Order Flow?

Investing in the stock market has been deemed to be a lucrative venture for many investors. However, it is good for an investor to have a prior understanding of how trade execution processes are carried out. When an investor contacts a brokerage firm for purposes of trading, various procedures and processes are undertaken by the broker to facilitate trade execution. It is important for investors to remember that brokers are also engaged in this business for purposes of making profits. This means that they are likely to follow procedures for order execution that will earn them revenue for every transaction they carry out.

One of the major sources of income for brokers is Payment for Order Flow. This basically refers to the amount of compensation that a broker receives for sending an order for particular party for purposes of execution. The stock market trade execution processes are so chained together that brokers and market makers have to work together to ensure a smooth flow of trade execution procedures.

A lot of enticing and marketing takes place especially towards brokers who have the responsibility of directing orders to their preferred trading partners for purposes of execution. When this happens, a brokerage firm usually gets a small payment to act as compensation for sending orders to a particular party. The revenue realized from this transaction is referred to payment for order flow. The value of this payment is usually calculated as a percentage of the value of the penny share.

Payment for order flow is actually a main source of revenue particularly for small brokerage firms that lack the capability to process thousands of orders. This allows brokers to pass on their orders to another firm which has the capability together with other orders carry out the best trade execution practices to guarantee the investor good gains on the market. For the broker, their cost of transactions is lowered substantially while market makers gain the advantage to deal with large volumes of shares in exchange for some form of compensation. Payment for Order Flow basically means that revenue brokers gain for directing traffic to specified market makers.

In this business, every entity has its own preferred trading partners. Just the same way a retailer chooses to only deal with specific suppliers in exchange of discounts on commodities purchases, the same concept applies in stock trade execution as stock brokers are at liberty to choose who will pass their orders to.

The SEC however has regulations that govern the administration of Payment for Order Flow to ensure that all trading procedures carried out are above board and ultimately benefit investors. SEC laws require brokers to furnish investors with information whenever they receive a payment for an order sent out to certain parties. This is a requirement should be facilitated on account opening and annually for every order that payment is successfully received.

Market makers understand too well that the only way to acquire several orders for trade execution is to woo brokers to direct orders to them. Market Makers always come up with a compensation package which they advertise to brokers in an attempt to increase order traffic. The plan could either be a penny or a higher price per penny stock share. Brokerage firms earn their income using this method or alternatively use the process of internalization to gain revenue.

The SEC rules are pretty clear – brokers are required to inform investors in the event that they receive payment for order flow. This information should be accompanied by a detailed account of the transactions and payments made. Customers in this case the investors have a right to make a request in writing to find out the source of the payments relating to a particular transaction.

All these regulations have been put in place to ensure brokers don't abuse Payment for Order flow to make unrealistically huge financial gains at the expense of the investor. This is important as all parties involved in the trade executions feel that transparency has been observed and all transactions have been executed above board. SEC policies aim to ensure that brokers don't get into deals that will exploit investors and endanger their investment.

It has been proved that Payment for Order Flow is a concept that is very much alive on Wall Street and other major stock trading platforms. The critical aspect is that as much as brokerage firms are trading to earn revenue for their operations, they need to do it in the best interest of their clients. Payment for Order Flow has no direct disadvantages to investors, in fact, some people have argued that it helps investors to secure the best trading execution deals.

Payment for Order Flow was launched by Bernard Madoff and has since generated a lot of controversy. Major gains were realized in 2009 with this process when the NYSE asked for permission from the U.S. Securities and Exchange Commission (S.E.C) to allow Payment for Order Flow to be included on its electronic exchange. The fluctuation of market prices particularly with penny stocks has caused the payment for order flow to reduce over the years.

Stock brokers are in business and therefore, they have to find ways to generate an income through their activities. While there are several ways of obtaining revenue in the trade execution process, brokerage firms seem to have a preference for payment for order flow and internalization. While it is perfectly fine for brokers to explore avenues of earning steady revenue, it is important to ensure that fair policies are put in place to safeguard investor interests.

As an investor, it is important to have some basic understanding about payment for order flow, what it is and how it is likely to influence the outcome of your trade execution orders. If you are in doubt what the term and its implications have on your investment, feel free to browse the internet or alternatively, you could discuss with your brokerage firm to have them shed more light on payment for order flow.

Chapter 7 (Section b)

What is a Limit Order?

There are several types of exchange orders that brokers can implement on behalf of the investor. It is important to note that the type of trade execution approach used has a large bearing on the benefits that an investor will accrue from a transaction. There are 2 main types of orders which are market order and limit order. Market orders allow for flexibility for factors such as price and time to execute orders influence the trade execution process.

A limit order places an emphasis on how an order should be handled particularly when it comes to the price. It basically means that a stock should only be sold or bought at a specific price usually referred to as the limit price. A limit order can either be a buy limit order or a sell limit order. In the case of a buy limit order, the investor sets a price within which they are willing to purchase a stock, this therefore means that an order can only be executed at the exact limit price or if it is lower. For instance, if a buyer sets the buy limit order price at $10 per share, the stock can only be purchased if the price per share is $10 or less.

In the case of a sell limit order, the opposite of a buy limit order applies. In this case, the order can only be executed if the limit price or higher is attained. It is important to note that a limit order has no guarantee to execute, it can only be declared a transaction once the limit price and the stock market value price match. Limit orders are beneficial to an investor particularly because they allow an investor to only spend an amount that is within their budget. This therefore means that if the market price doesn't meet the expectations of an investor, the order cannot be filled for trading.

What makes a limit order unique is the fact that it is not same as a market order. No execution can take place unless the necessary set limit price is achieved. Time is a factor because an order cannot remain open forever, if the limit price cannot be attained within the period an order is remains outstanding, it has to be cancelled. The whole idea behind a limit order is to ensure that an investor is not forced to pay extra than what they had budgeted for.

There are specified conditions that govern the operation of limit orders. FOK order commonly known as Fill or Kill order happens when an investor issues instructions that if their order fails to be filled then it must be cancelled with immediate effect. Another condition could require all the shares to be bought or sold executed in a single transaction or within the same timeframe (all or none order).

Limit orders are more expensive that market orders because industry players know they are tricky to fill. The advantage of these orders is that they allow investors realize the amount they had initially indicated before execution. Many investors prefer using limit order particularly on stocks that are considered highly volatile or trading on low volumes. A limit order potentially reduces risks associated with market uncertainty as an investor has the freedom to choose the limits within which they wish to trade. Before going for a limit order, it is good to research and evaluate the implications this decision will have on your trade execution procedures. Before opting for a limit order, an investor should weigh in on their options and possibly seek for a professional interpretation of this decision from their broker.

Chapter Seven (Section c)

What is a Market Order?

In order to facilitate trading within the stock exchange markets, an order has to be placed for purposes of trade execution. As an investor, you have the right to choose how you want your orders to be executed. Currently, there are 2 main types of orders; market order and limit order. Each order has its own characteristics and rules that govern the way a transaction will be carried out.

Our focus is to specifically discuss a market order, what it is, how to place market orders and the circumstances under which they are used. When an investor instructs a broker to sell their stock at the best available market price, the trade transaction that is executed is known as a market order. Actually, it is the default and most commonly used order on the stock market. One important characteristic of a market order is that it has no restriction since the main aim is to find the best current price for the stock. Unlike a limit order, the lack of restrictions on price and trading time frames makes it an easier order to execute. A market order can either be a buy or sell order depending on the transaction an investor wishes to execute. 'Unrestricted order' is another name used to refer to a market order.

The reason why market orders are common is because there is a guarantee of execution. The lack of restrictions allows room for freedom of trading so long as ultimate execution process generates profit for the investor. This order doesn't attract high commissions because the process involved in executing the order is fairly simple and doesn't require a lot of work. However, it's important for industry players to avoid pegging market orders to stocks that are characterized with low average trading prices. This is because chances are usually high that the ask price an investor is looking for could be higher than the current market price. This causes a large spread, something that isn't good for an investor since they might be forced to spend more on stocks than they had originally anticipated. High volume stocks are always the best option for investors who want to make good money from market orders.

Nowadays, we have various technologies that have been incorporated into stock market trading. When an investor orders for a buy or sell transaction, the order is placed in a system that arranges several orders in a specific order for purposes of execution. The rules for order processing have already been defined in the computer based systems which then use a variety of parameters mainly the price to determine the order of execution. Investors who request for a market order have typically agreed that their stock can be executed at whichever market price is available, this significantly reduces the execution time as orders are executed based on the current stock market prices.

The administration of market orders is fairly simple, it all depends on how much an investor is asking for whenever they want to buy or sell a stock. In other words, the processing system usually arranges stock prices according to the price. For instance, if you wish to buy stocks, the best bid price for a particular stock is usually placed at the top of the processing system meaning it is executed before others. For selling stocks, the best ask price takes the top position on the column. When orders are sent into the system, the orders with the best prices are filled first. Should an order with a better price be sent in, it moves straight to the top and dislodges the ones that previously occupied the top position.

The market works this way – investors who place the highest prices to buy stocks always win the order whereas those selling their stocks for the lowest price sell them before others. While market orders are known to be quite popular with stock trading, you need to be careful when trading with them. Slippage is a fee an investor has to pay on market orders particularly if the market maker becomes mischievous and decides change the spread in order to make higher profits. This practice is discouraged but market makers still go ahead to make investors pay for small premiums which ultimately increase the profit for the market maker. Slippage refers to the variation of the bid ask spread when an order is entered to the time it gets filled. Market makers usually cause changes to the price upsetting it for their own business gains and interests.

The next important issue we need to discuss is when one should use market orders. The stock market is highly volatile and sometimes things can go wrong or right within a split of a second. As an investor, when you feel there is a danger of losing out on trading on particular stocks, you must find a quick way to exit before more damage is done. Every investor has the responsibility of safeguarding their investment and this means reacting quickly in cases that could jeopardize an investment. One concern that comes up is the issue of slippage; many investors become a worried lot particular because they are aware they have no power to control stock entry and exit prices. Slippage may initially seem like losing out on a few cents, however, in the long run investors could end up losing quite a significant amount of their investment.

What happens when placing Market Orders?

Once you instruct your stock broker to buy or sell shares for you, many factors that could have a final influence on the price you eventually receive begin taking shape. For both buying and selling orders, actively traded stocks guarantee you the best opportunity for your order to get filed almost immediately. However, when there is too much activity on the stock, the price that you entered the stock with might not be necessarily what you will receive. However, in most cases, one usually gets the best price close to what they had asked for not unless other dramatic changes to the price occur.

The stock markets traditionally allow investors with the highest buy order to quickly get sell orders while buyers offering the lowest sell order quickly find buy orders.

Chapter Seven (Section d)

What is the Ask Price?

When it comes to stock trading, it is a great idea to learn terms that are used in stock trading. One of the terms that you need to understand is ask price. What is the ask price? Well, ask price is also referred to as list price. Ask price is the price a seller lists for items they wish to sell. Most of the time, you will hear the term asking price referred to the cost of purchase. It is good to know that ask price is usually more than a person is expecting to get for something, unless they are asking low so as to promote a quick sale. In most cases, asking price is the point at which you begin negotiations and bargaining on an actual price. In simple terms, ask price is the lowest price at which a seller is willing to sell their stock or bond. It is always important to compare the bid price so as to calculate the spread. Most of the time, a seller is willing to sell their stock in exchange for a specific security.

When the stock market is hot the ask price usually increase. This always becomes challenging to get a person selling their bond to come down in price. When the demand for buying stocks exceeds those available in the stock market, interests buyers are forced to exceed their ask price in order to buy the stock. In a stable stock market or when the market deflates, there is much more bargaining room. A qualified and experienced stock broker can help one to determine an affordable asking price offer for the bonds.

This does not guarantee that your ask price will be accepted and you will need to research more to find the right appropriate offer. If you quote that is below the asking price, chances are high that you will not get the stocks. On the other hand, if there are no more offers on the table, the seller may counter offer with the amount still lower than the ask price but higher than your offer. For people who choose not to consult a stock broker, it will be a great idea to look at different stock trading sites to see how much the ask price is selling. It is also possible to submit an offer thorough these stock trading sites. If the seller turns up something relevant that reduces the value of the home, this information can help one lower your offer.

In determining offers on a product list price, there different ways you can use to guide you in letting you know the high and low prices that befit you. This is particularly helpful w you are purchasing a product. When you purchase a product, you may also want to consider what it the list price might be in a few years you plan to sell the product. It is good to know that the market uses different prices for products and high resale values can priced accordingly. As a buyer you need to be aware if these trends can help you to decide on how much bargaining power you possess.

How does the ask price work? While the ask price is at it's the lowest price, a potential seller is willing to accept, the bid price is the highest price that a potential buyer is willing to pay for the security. You should know that the highest bid and lowest ask price are quoted a many exchanges and the difference between prices is known as bid ask spread. When a potential investor decides wants to sell a security, he doesn't need to offer it at the market price and instead he can use the limit order to specify to his order that he wants to sell the security as long as its surpasses the particular price.

Most of the time, the ask price of a specific security is usually displayed in quote services such as Yahoo Finance as the lowest ask price in the market. However, the investors don't need to buy or sell securities at these prices. Potential investors are allowed to specify their bid price when telling their broker to start a trade. It is good to know that the trade may not be executed instantly but the seller can be assured that they will not make less than they initially invested.

Chapter Eight

Where Can I Find Quoted Prices for Stock I Am Trading in the OTC Market?

We are living in an internet age where finding information has become quite easy thanks to the numerous online platforms in existence today. The stock market industry has today become one of the most sought after investment ventures for people looking to expand their financial fortune. Before getting into this investment, you need to have a good idea of what goes on behind the scenes and seek proper advice from industry experts before making any major decisions. Remember, this is your investment and you wouldn't want to do anything rush that could jeopardize your efforts.

Understanding the difference between major exchange counters and OTC otherwise known as "Over the Counter" transactions is very important. Apart from formal security exchanges for instance NYSE, TSX and AMEX, we have alternative trading platforms that investors can use to transact and grow the value of their investment. OTC stocks trade on the sidelines of major exchanges and are usually characterized by a dealer network as opposed to major exchanges that revolve around a centralized system of operations.

OTC markets are usually relevant because the trade that goes on here is associated mainly with smaller firms that are unable to meet larger exchange listing demands. Unlisted stocks are a common term used to refer to these securities that entail brokers and dealers making direct negotiations on various transactions. This can be done over the internet or using other communication gadgets such as phones. It's important to mention that NASDAQ is classified as a dealer network though its stocks are not classified as OTC since the platform is a fully fledged exchange.

If you intend to know the value of your stocks on the OTC market, you should know that these stocks trade Over the Counter Bulletin Board (OTCBB) or Pink Sheets. One word of caution though, you need to be careful when trading because some of the stocks you see on the OTCBB could have been sponsored by firm with bad credit history. Financial derivatives such as bonds don't find their way on major stock exchange markets and therefore trade on OTC counters. For instance one good way of knowing the quotes for a bond on the OTC counter is to contact the bank responsible for creating the market for the bond and directly requesting for the quotes.

As mentioned earlier, the role of technology has played a big part in relaying information especially on quotes on OTC counters to the relevant parties involved in the transaction. The OTC link is a popular electronic inter-dealer quotation system that publishes quotes from brokers and dealers plying their trade in different OTC securities. Brokers and dealers engaged in the buying and selling process of securities on OTC platforms usually use these facilities to make public their bid and ask prices. OTC is recognized as an alternative trading system having obtained and meet registration requirements from the SEC. Due to the relaxed nature of listing requirements, several small companies or thinly traded stocks find this platform quite ideal.

While on the internet, you will realize that you can never fall short of platforms to give you information on quoted market prices on OTC markets. There are several electronic online system developed by various companies that provide investors with real time information of what is happening on the market. It is good to note that platforms such as Yahoo Finance have played an instrumental role in providing investors with real time information on stock prices trading on the OTC counters. Yahoo Finance gives investors a chance to see what is happening on the markets as well as come up with crucial decisions on how transactions need to be executed.

Understanding how ticker symbols work and how to interpret their use is very important. Ticker symbol is an abbreviation of a particular stock on the counter. Using ticker symbols, an investor should easily identify the stocks they are interested in and monitor how they are currently performing on the market. The internet has presented so many opportunities that you can use to keep an eye on how the stocks are performing. Whether you have stocks on mainstream exchanges or OTC counters, you have the right to access information that concerns your investment.

If you can't find or interpret information found on the internet, you should seek the assistance of a broker to get advice on how to effectively monitor prices on OTC markets. Having an idea on market quoted prices is crucial as it enables you as an investor to strategize and plan on how to grow your investment. OTC markets have on some occasions been associated with fraud and other dubious deals, keeping an eye on quoted prices and other important parameters lets increases the level of transparency.

OTC markets have introduced an easier and more flexible way of allowing investors to trade various securities. There is need to ensure transparency when it comes to finding information current quoted prices on the OTC markets. You don't have to worry about finding out issues regarding price particularly considering there is plenty of technology supported platforms that fetch this information from OTC platforms. You need to have this information in order to make any critical decisions that will determine how well you will grow your investment.

Keeping up with platforms that constantly reflect changes on the stock market is the best way to stay updated. You need to be more proactive in sourcing for channels that will avail you information which is accurate and within the shortest time possible. Getting discrepancies on quoted stock prices could be misleading and lead to wrong decision making. Luckily, most of the technologies available are spot on when it comes to getting information from OTC markets and disseminating it to investors who want to know quoted prices. Both large stock exchanges and OTC counters rely on real time technology facilities to relay information on quoted stock prices to both investors as well as all parties involved in the trade execution process.

Chapter Eight (Section a)

Where Can I check How My Penny Stocks Are Trading?

Investing in the stock market has been found to be appealing by most investors who are looking to widen their investments through stock trading. The risks are there and investors understand too well that success depends on how vigilant you are especially when it comes to monitoring trading transactions. Before investing in this business, you need to research and figure out how you will be able to get firsthand information on any transactions happening on the floor of the exchange. With the current technology developments, the industry has opened up various information channels for the purposes of keeping investors informed about their penny stock trading.

As an investor, it is your right to get access to real-time accurate information particularly regarding penny stocks you have worked so hard to invest in. We all desire to have some good level of transparency and accountability particularly when we put our money into an investment venture. Nowadays, there are several ways that you can use to keep an eye on the stocks. This is important as various factors causes price changes which could ultimately influence some decisions that you make.

The use of charts has gained momentum in the recent past particularly for those who want to keep an eye on penny stock prices. Charts have become a clear favorite particularly due to the fact that they have a strong sense of visual representation that makes it easy to interpret figures. Tracking and analyzing of penny stocks using pictures is quite advantageous as it enables you to enjoy high speeds of acquiring information, ease of use as well as clarity of information presentation.

These charts give you information in the simplest manner and therefore anyone can be able to quickly interpret this information and know what it means. There are several online charting services that you can use to monitor your penny stocks. So far, BigChart has been proved to be one of the best and simplest charting services to relay information on stock trading transactions.

If you carry out your trade using a broker, you can get current penny stock quotes through your broker's website. For this reason, it is important to make sure that you choose an established brokerage firm that has the required technology resources to keep you informed particularly in regards to your penny stock investment. It is also possible to use platforms such as BigCharts to access penny stock quotes as well as their respective charts. The internet is an ideal platform with several resources that investors can use to monitor the stock markets.

You can obtain information on quotes from tools such as Yahoo Finance that keep a detailed and accurate account of how penny stocks are performing on the market. Learning how to set alerts and interpret this information is crucial particularly if you want to receive timely updates on stock price quotes. There is plenty of technology at your disposal that you can use to find penny stock quotes within the shortest time possible, learning how to use these facilities is key.

If you decide to invest in stocks, you must ensure that you stay updated with the current industry news. With this investment, you must be ready to source for news particularly headlines that will either directly or indirectly affect the value of stocks on the market. A number of public companies that deal with penny stocks are always in the news for various reasons. Occasionally, there are press releases that are meant to inform the public particularly shareholders on important new and events related to the company.

Are you curious to see how your penny stocks are trading? Using a portfolio monitor allows you to keep an eye on several penny stocks simultaneously. Having an edge when it comes to acquiring accurate information is very critical in this business. Keeping an eye on your picks allows you to be confident knowing the fact that you have every detail of all transactions happening and how they could affect the value of your penny stocks. If you have several investment plans, a portfolio monitor allows you to do this with so much convenience. This in turn makes it very easy and quick to source for trading opportunities and how you can achieve maximum gain from them. Yahoo Finance Portfolio is particularly helpful in availing information on the current market trends.

Penny stock profiles have been helpful particularly for investors looking for a reliable methodology to keep an eye on their penny stocks. The advantage of using profiles is that they are very detailed in terms of information. A snapshot of the firm, its model as well as important trading statistics are usually included in this profile.

Please note that each profile varies depending on the source for similar penny stocks. CBS Market Watch Profile and Yahoo Finance Profile are some of the places you can have a detailed profile. For instance, to get a Yahoo Finance Profile, you first need to obtain the quote then select 'profile' to access the information.

Penny stock message boards can be used to relay important information. However, they can sometimes misinform you about crucial financial data because the information issued out is always conflicting. There are so many message boards out there and so knowing which one provides the most accurate information is a challenge.

Before investing your money in penny stocks, just make sure to research and find out how you will be monitoring your stocks. With such kind of an investment, regular and precise updates are absolutely important to let you know which direction your investment is headed. As a matter of fact, you need to have this information at your fingertips before making any move. So if you are planning to spend money on stocks, issues of how you are monitoring your investment need to be decided upon. Trading in penny stocks is one of the best investment ventures you can consider particularly if you are keen to begin small. With proper platforms to monitor your investment, you should be able to realize sound financial returns.

Chapter Eight (Section b)

How Do I Know the Penny Stock That I Am Considering Investing in is Not Fraudulent?

Many people are nowadays considering establishing their financial base early in life. This has led to an increased demand for investment ventures such as the stock market where people can put their money with the hope of regaining back their investment coupled with handsome profits. Penny stocks have become very common and therefore you need to be careful and learn not to get into schemes that will jeopardize your financial investment. Lack of information and ignorance has been responsible for the misery of many penny stock investors. This in turn causes investors to get duped and end up losing their hard earned to dubious schemes set up for personal and selfish interests.

Research is critical particularly if you are keen on getting the right information that will guide you to make informed choices. Penny stocks can be highly rewarding though they are also known to be very volatile. A number of scams such as pump and dump have also hit the penny stock market causing investors to lose a lot of money through dubious investment schemes engineered by unscrupulous people out to make profits from unsuspecting investors. It is your responsibility to make sure that you purchase penny stocks from trustworthy sources. This means that you must research and know what to avoid. In case you need professional help, you can always consult with a brokerage firm just to get an assurance that your intended penny stock investment is legitimate.

To begin with, you must have adequate information about the company you intend to invest in. This means that you need to avoid companies whose annual revenue margins do not meet the required threshold. Ideally, investors are advised to keep off firms whose annual revenue is less than $ 10 million. A number of investors have been caught up in scams because of investing in firms that are not well established in their line of operation. Having knowledge of the company you are investing in is also a wise idea. Investors are always advised not to put their money in firms whose operations and chain of business they don't understand. When you invest in such a company, you lack the capacity to develop strong oversight ability since you have no clear understanding of what the business does. In such cases, firms could easily find leeway to engage in corporate multipractice at the expense of investors who have bought shares with the company.

It is also good to purchase stocks with companies you are genuinely interested in. Chances are high that you or your stock broker will notice suspicious trading patterns particularly with a firm you are well versed and have experience with. Its natural, we tend to be more careful with things we love and have interest in. The process of avoiding to invest in fraudulent stocks needs to be initiated from the beginning. You need to be careful and understand the type of penny stock you are putting your money.

As much as advertising is not bad for penny stocks, you must be absolutely careful about unsolicited emails that are sent to you promoting penny stocks from certain companies. In most cases, this happens when promoters are contracted to engage in a vigorous advertising campaign that sends out emails. The only disadvantage with this is that some unscrupulous dealers have used this system to dupe investors by creating a fake hype to give an impression that the penny stocks are very lucrative. As a matter of fact, quite a number of investors have lost their hard earned money to this type of dubious investments. The lesson is – don't fully trust adverts sent to you via email promoting certain types of stocks. In fact, it's better to keep off completely and carry out independent research with the help of professionals to identify the right type of penny stocks to invest in.

These days, everyone has employed all manner of tactics with an aim of marketing penny stocks to investors. Differentiating between real genuine penny stocks and frauds can be very tricky. Don't believe everything you read on email particularly if you haven't officially subscribed to an email listing service. Marketing emails usually originate from sources you don't know and cannot ostensibly prove their authenticity.

The trading platforms for penny stocks are clear and well known. Therefore, don't buy stocks that trade on exchanges you have no idea about. Besides the mainstream exchanges like NYSE, penny stocks use bulletin boards and OTC (Over-the-counter) for trading purposes. You should be very skeptical particularly if you come across a stock that is not trading on any of the above mentioned platforms. This could be a sign to show that possibilities of the stock being fraudulent are actually valid. Before purchasing any penny stocks, do a refined search and verify the trading platforms for the stock you intend to purchase.

Looking out for signs of a possible fraudulent stock can be quite simple particularly if you are keen to look at all the critical aspects involved in purchasing a penny stock. If you realize that a particular penny stock is being advertised too much, you need to raise the red flag. Well organized schemes go to the extent of paying dishonest writers to discuss certain penny stocks in a positive light. Fake press releases have in the past been released to give the market an impression that particular penny stocks are the best choice for investors.

If you are quite keen, you should be able on your own to notice suspicious signs of a fraudulent penny stock. It is your responsibility to ensure that no monetary commitments are made before verification that a stock you intend to invest in is genuine. Many regulatory bodies have put in place measures to ensure that fraudulent traders are denied the chance to fleece unsuspecting penny stock investors of their money. Exercising care and talking to industry professionals about the available options is the best way to go.

Chapter Eight (Section c)

Should I Worry When Buying Shares of Penny Stocks That Has Declared Bankruptcy?

As an investor interested in penny stocks, you need to learn all about stocks before investing in them. If you are thinking about buying penny stocks that have been declared bankruptcy you need to be careful. Betting on stocks that have been declared bankruptcy has become common in stock trading and rise rapidly once the companies emerge from bankruptcy. It is important to know that if a company has filed for bankruptcy, chances are that penny stocks will become worthless with time. What many shareholders don't know is the owners of these companies under bankruptcy protection are usually the last people in line for claims on assets. To explain further, if you are a shareholder, don't have high expectations. Although the company may come out of bankruptcy it will most likely cancel its existing equity shares.

Some people who invest in these stocks are shareholders locking their losses for tax purposes. Also, you need to know that some of the trading is likely being carried out by investors who don't know what they are doing. You need to know that when companies are unable to meet the listing requirements to trade on NASDAQ they get delisted. However, their shares continue to trade Over the Counter

Bulletin Board (OTCBB) or Pink Sheets. It is good to know that stock bankruptcy companies have letter Q at the end of their ticker symbol. When you visit Pink Sheet Website and search the symbols for such a company, a red warning comes up with the link to SEC site with info on corporate bankruptcy. Therefore, as an investor, you need to be cautious when buying penny stock of companies that have been declared bankruptcy because it is extremely risky and can likely lead to financial loss.

When a penny stocks company goes bankrupt, the investors holding the stocks or bonds are affected. If you are still wondering if buying stock of a bankrupt company is a good idea, you need to know that bankruptcy is not good for bond owners and stockholders. However, some companies have emerged from bankruptcy stronger and able to continue with operations. Bankruptcy is a form of liquidation under the federal law. The bankruptcy law covers both individuals and companies although there are many differences.

Many stock trading experts advise investors to avoid buying shares of penny stocks that has been declared bankruptcy. When a company files for bankruptcy protection, court oversees. A lot of claims of people and entities that are owned money come first, and then stockholders come last. If there are preferred stock owners, they come before common shares. The order for priority for claims is approximated from tax owned, wage owned, trade creditors, bank lenders and preferred stock.

In many cases, if the company emerges from a bankruptcy process it will issue new common stock. In most bankruptcies, one of the main reasons for corporate failure is use of too much leverage. In order to keep operating the company should stop paying a lot of interest on debts and dividends on preferred stock. At this point, the court converts old debt and preferred stock to new common shares.

For common stock to be cancelled from bankruptcy there is need for net assets left over after the claims of higher claimants are satisfied. Initially, if a bankrupt company had good obligations, it will not need to declare bankruptcy. Nowadays, there are reports in the financial press of optimistic individual investors who choose stock companies in bankruptcy. One of the reasons why it is not a great idea to invest in buying shares of penny stocks that has declared bankruptcy is the fact that common shareholders are wiped out completely. Banks and bond holders are usually given new common stock at the beginning of trading after the court protection is over. As an investor, you need to know that old common stocks cancelled become worthless forever. Old common shares trade at very low prices compared to new common stocks. Therefore, when you see a former bankrupt company stocks being quoted again at a high price do not be deceived.

Just in case of a bankruptcy of financial institutions such as bank or brokers, it is rare that anything can possibly be left to common owners. Well, assets held are usually worthless than they are indicated on the books. Also, the leverage involved means that there little losses on assets that are magnified in terms of depleting remaining equity. Another thing is that most preferred stocks are usually 100 cents on the $. That is if there is anything left for the common owner which is highly unlikely. You also need to know that lawyers, accounts and consultants will also need to get paid before the shareholders. Penny stock experts advise investors to avoid buying shares of penny stocks that has declared bankruptcy. You should not try to get your hopes high on such stocks hoping a miracle will happen. If you happen to own such stocks, the best thing you can do is to sell them before trading stops and you end up closing sale transaction for tax purposes.

You need to know that penny stock trading is risky and this is the reason that you need to take it slow. Although trading penny stocks is very easy, cheap and straight forward, you need to take time so as not to lose money. The fact that you can make money from penny stocks trading fast also makes them a great ground for scammers. Many investors who decide to get into penny stock trading without taking enough time to research and understand how to trade become victims of scammers. Also they end up losing a lot of money by buying penny stock shares that has been declared bankruptcy. As an investor, you need to research on the internet on trading penny stocks. Alternatively, you can use a broker to guide you through. What you need to remember is to avoid getting entangled into buying shares of penny stocks that has been declared bankruptcy.

Chapter Eight (Section d)

Why Do Penny Stocks Change So Much?

When you make the decision to invest in penny stocks, you must be aware that price changes are bound to occur. Frequent price fluctuations are a common scenario in the stock market industry and you shouldn't be surprised when this happens. Just like mainstream stocks, penny stocks are also affected by the same market factors that trigger a change in stock prices. This is one reality that penny stock investors need to be aware of before committing financially to the stock market. Investors wish that prices could always be on an upward trend but unfortunately, this does not happen every time. Certain market factors could make penny stock prices take a deep dive.

Before investing in penny stocks, you should take some time and evaluate which factors could trigger price fluctuations. The technicality here should be to determine how you can use these factors to make any substantial financial gains. Top selling stocks also go through turbulent times and as an investor, you must be prepared for days of celebrations and disappointments. Every day, we witness huge price differences in stocks based on several events and various market factors. Wise investors need to have strong foresight and brace themselves for major decisions in event of any changes.

When you choose to buy penny stocks, you should know that just like any other investment, supply and demand are and will always be factors that you need to watch out for. Each day, the stock market goes through several hurdles which in turn have a great bearing on stock prices. When supply increases, stock prices slump as many traders are usually in the process of selling their stocks. When the market gets too flooded with sellers, be prepared to see your penny stocks lose value. However, the demand for penny stocks increases when more buyers become interested to purchase the stocks. When this happens, prices are forced to go up and therefore investors keen on selling their stocks at this instance can make maximum profits. Research has also revealed that consumer confidence also can also influence the factors of supply and demand.

If you are dealing with penny stocks, be advised that prices will always change for various reasons. Over time, it has been proved that the release of a company's financial reports usually triggers a price change in penny stocks. Earnings reports always reflect a firm's performance and its financial status. If the company releases strong reports, stock prices usually respond to the announcement with a price increment. It is important to know that listed companies are usually required to release quarterly reports. This information particularly helps investors who want to know how the companies they have invested in are performing financially.

Business environments sometimes change rapidly and as a penny stock investor, you have to be prepared for changes in the corporate scene. Of course, business entities exist to compete for the largest share of the market. However, some businesses are usually forced to merge or are taken over by other companies. Stock markets are known to be very volatile particularly when rumors of corporate changes start doing their rounds. Takeovers and mergers cause elicit different reactions from the stock market. Depending on the reasons of the new business partnerships, penny stock prices could either go up or down. So, whenever you hear about an impending merger or takeover, get braced for stock market price changes.

We live in a world where events are taking place every single moment. The stock market is known to always directly respond to various events of a varied nature. Political, social and economic factors have the capability to influence penny stock prices. It is important to note that news events that directly relate to a company you have purchased penny stocks from will always affect the price values. For many investors, good news comes when penny stock prices appreciate in value. However, bad news always negatively affects penny stock prices. Issues such as political instability, insecurity and disasters always cause a slump in penny stock prices. In simple terms, news that affects a company positively causes an increase in stock prices. On the other hand, bad news for a company could spell doom for stock prices. Events happening in competitor companies also contribute to penny stock price variations. Cases in point include instances when a competitor firm successfully acquires a patent to develop and distribute a particular product.

Several countries both developed and developing economies are grappling with the problem of unemployment. You might not realize this but high unemployment rates have a negative impact on the entire stock market. Whether you are penny stock or large cap investor, people not getting hired is not good for the stock market. Countries with high rates of unemployment record lower levels of economic achievement because a large majority of the population is not making money to sustain themselves. On the other hand, countries with low unemployment rates have a more stable and attractive stock market. If you live in a country that is experiencing high unemployment rates, penny stock prices could be drastically affected.

If you think the local stock market is not influenced by global events, you are mistaken. When you decide to become a penny stock investor, global events directly affect the value of your investment. This means that even if you have invested in a small local company, anything that happens on the global scene should be of concern to you. Cases such as terrorism acts have seriously affected global stock market prices. When events of such magnitude happen, stocks markets are affected on a global level.

Penny stocks globally have been affected by pump and dump scams which have cost investors their hard earned cash. Cases have been witnessed where unscrupulous traders usually insiders create rumors that cause the demand for penny stocks to increase. This dupes several investors to purchase stocks at high prices because of the high demand. These same clique of insiders then decide to offset their shares in bulk netting huge profits. When this happens, the market becomes over flooded causing penny stocks prices to immediately drop. Penny stock investors who fall for this trick always end up making huge losses while the masterminds of the scheme smile all the way to the bank.

Sometimes, companies decide to buy back stocks from the public due to various reasons. When this happens, shares still available on the market cause a rise in demand thus causing stock prices to increase substantially.

There are several factors that cause penny stock prices to change. When engaging in this investment, just be sure to understand that stock markets could either work in your favor or work against you. Due to several market factors, news and events, it is impossible to keep stock prices at a constant level. Whether you choose to invest in penny stocks or large cap stocks, you should brace yourself of upward and downward trends in stock prices depending on the prevailing market conditions. In case you want to learn and understand more about how stock markets react, the internet is a good source that can help you to understand changes that you should anticipate as a penny stock investor.

Lack of understanding on why penny stock prices change so much can lead to disappointments especially for investors who engage in this investment hoping to become rich in a short period of time. When investing in penny stock prices, just make sure that you have a thorough understanding of how the market operates. Please, make sure that you are not here to make overnight riches as you will end up very disappointed. Investors who understand why penny stock prices change get an opportunity to make good decisions that will safeguard their investments and allow financial prosperity.

Chapter Eight (Section e)

Can I Make Money with a Buy and Hold Strategy?

Investment has a lot of theories with each advancing a particular point of argument on how investors can maximum returns. The approach you decide to use when investing in the stock market needs to be well informed and selected based on factors and a critical analysis of industry trends. Investors use different strategies to try and maximize the value of their investment in the stock market industry. Ideally, there are 2 major approaches to stock trading- you can choose to participate actively in trading or opt for a more laid back Buy and Hold strategy. Selection of an approach to use depends on several factors which largely revolve around the personality of an individual investing in the stock markets.

Active trading means as an investor you are in the business on a day to day basis, monitoring and analyzing the market as well as making crucial decisions on how to obtain maximum returns. When you choose Buy and Hold strategy, you basically make an investment in the stock market mainly to for extended periods of time. In such a case, you are not concerned about immediate or current shakeups in the stock market industry as well as the impact they have on the stock market. This is ideally a long term investment and therefore many investors don't keep an eye on technical indicators that have the capability of shifting market trends.

Various arguments have been fronted particularly with an aim of establishing whether buy and hold strategy is better than participating in the stock market as an active participant. When you look at both strategies, each of them has its own disadvantages and pitfalls. So, if you are trying to understand whether you can earn a good investment from Buy and Hold strategy, a sustainable approach would be to critically evaluate the advantages of opting for a buy and hold strategy.

If you are considering a sustainable long term stock investment venture, you should consider the buy and hold strategy and the advantages it has offer. In case you are keen on a well diversified investment and to save costs and the stress associated with daily monitoring of stock markets, the buy and hold strategy might be the best solution for you.

The advantage that many investors who decide to go for buy and hold investment acquire is that it is simpler to understand the details of stock markets particularly when you decide to invest for long periods of time. This is because long term investments save you the hassle of understanding the technicalities involved with the day to day management of stock market investments.

Buy and hold strategies are anchored in the investment theory and therefore making it a better idea in the long run. Dealing with stocks that are highly volatile could sometimes demand for time in order to allow the markets to recover from various challenges that could have negatively influenced stock prices.

Many investors prefer buy and hold investment approach as opposed to active participation in day to day stock activities. This approach enables you to maintain soberness as well as cultivate a more disciplined approach when it comes to decision making regarding stock markets. Not having to worry about current stock price fluctuations due to various market factors contributes to a more disciplined strategy and adoption of wise long term trading strategies.

When you engage less in active stock trading practices, chances of making huge savings particularly in terms of transaction fees becomes a clear advantage. Investors who opt to keep their stocks active on the market for extended periods of time enjoy lower costs of keeping their stocks on the market. This is important as saving allows you to have extra cash that can be put into other profitable investment ventures. You need to understand that the more you engage in trading, the more money you have to spend to remain relevant on the market. The issue of taxation is also critical for those who prefer adopt the buy and hold approach. Investors who keep their stock investments for a long period of time enjoy tax incentives which in turn substantially reduce their cost of savings.

In the long run, it is up to you to decide which option you want to use when investing in the stock market. You need to carry out extensive research and identify whether buy and hold or actively participating in the stock market is your best investment choice. You cannot afford to ignore evaluation of the benefits as well as pitfalls of each approach in before coming up with any decisions. Having discussed this topic from a broad perspective, there are tangible benefits of opting for Buy and Hold strategy especially for investors who want to realize substantial financial rewards.

Chapter Eight (Section f)

How Do I Find Out More About the People Running the Penny Stock Company?

The decision to invest in the stock markets should be approached with a lot of caution. Whilst there are many public out there offering the public a chance to own a piece of the company, it's your responsibility as an investor to research widely about a company before putting in your money. The stock market provides investors with a perfect opportunity to earn good returns from their investment. However, this can only be achieved if the right investment choices are made from the beginning.

Public companies are complex entities to run and therefore need a steady and well informed management team to handle the affairs of the company. There is a direct relationship between how a company is managed and the financial results posted on the markets to entice new investors. Good management practices and policies are absolutely essential for a company that wishes to realize substantial expansion in all its core areas of business. As an investor, you have the right to know how a company you intend to invest in is managed and who the key decision makers are.

The corporate sector especially public companies trading on the stock market are required for example to publish their financial reports for the general public to see and evaluate. The affairs of most of these companies get to the public's attention and it's therefore easy for one to have information on the people in charge of the firm. It's only natural that you would want to know who is handling your investment.

Penny stocks have become popular particularly due to the fact that it is easy for an investor to get a share of the company at a very low cost. One important point to mention is that many large companies that trade huge stocks initially began with penny stocks and worked to increase their value into the stock they are today.

Any firm that issues an offer for investors to purchase penny stocks is required by the law to provide information which includes the names of management staff involved in day to day running of the company. By doing this, there is a lot of transparency that enables prospective investors to have a better understanding of who owns the company. There are CEO's and managers of public firms who have been associated with exemplary performance and experience particularly in managing large public firms. As an investor, you are better off having your penny stocks in a well-managed company that gives you an assurance that your investment will be managed well.

With the current information dispensation and high levels of technology, we no longer have secrets particularly when it comes to management and running of public companies. To begin with, the internet is a useful platform that gives investors more information about a firm they wish to invest penny stocks. Firms that deal with publicly traded stocks have established websites where anyone wishing to invest in penny stocks has substantial information about the company.

Many of us are keen to know who is going to manage our money. Remember, if you put your investment in a company that is not well managed, there's a lot at stake. The chances of making any meaningful gains on your financial investment become less. There is a lot of emphasis particularly for people running penny stock companies to be well qualified and experienced. Many first time investors begin their journey in the stock market by investing in penny stocks. It is therefore good to make sure that their hard earned investment is safeguarded at all costs.

It's natural to want to find out about who manages a company before making your investment. A majority of stock trading transactions involve stock brokers who carry out trade executions based on instructions from the clients. Before investing in penny stocks, use your broker as a source of information to know more about the management of companies involved with penny stocks. Using your stock broker is a brilliant idea as they are practicing their trade in the industry and therefore have accurate insider information that might not get to the public domain. Brokers usually have an analysis of companies publicly trading their stocks both in terms of performance and management.

As an investor, these are critical issues that you need to watch out for before making an investment. They say "information is power" so getting plenty of industry information is good particularly if you want to understand more about the running of penny stock companies. When you purchase penny stocks, you give out your investment to the company to manage it for the purpose of increasing value and bringing profits. Information sourced from brokerage firms is very useful particularly for the making the decision of the best company to use for penny stock investment.

The media also plays an important role in informing the public about news related to the stock markets and companies trading on major exchange platforms. It is essential to know that the media provides an opportunity that sets the stage for the public to have information on companies that are currently trading on the stock market. Nowadays, we have several media platforms such as T.V. magazines, financial journals etc. that allow the society to learn about more about the people in charge of management of public companies. Large public companies that perform impressively on the exchange are easily recognizable and therefore attract a lot of attention from media. As an investor, it is then quite easy for you to access management information that can help you know and understand who is in charge of running the business.

As an investor, you should learn how to watch out for any information related to the stock markets that can be of benefit to your investment. Of course, research on people who run a penny stock company is information that you need to have well in advance before committing your finances. The methods and channels discussed above are the best for finding information about the management and running of penny stock companies.

Chapter Nine

What Are the Penny Stock Investment Fraud "RED FLAGS" to Look Out For?

Most investors put their money in penny stocks and forget the crucial role of monitoring to see how their stocks are performing. If you are planning to invest in penny stocks, you should know that the real work comes in when you have to spend time keeping a close eye on the market. This is not only to monitor the share price and trading patterns but also just to make sure that nothing sinister that can affect your investment goes on without your knowledge. In the recent past, some penny stocks have been associated with fraud raising questions of the need to have investor participation in watching over their stock investments.

To avoid getting into the trap of dubious schemes and gambling your hard earned income, investors should be on the lookout for RED FLAGS that indicate that all is not well. The internet has a lot of information that you can use to determine if there is problem and what course of action can be taken to avert further damage. Frauds are almost impossible to detect and if you are not vigilant, you might realize too late when the damage has already been done. There are several pointers that can make you suspect something isn't right, when this happens, it's time to wake up and get a reaction plan. Red flags are usually an indication of an impending penny stock scam carefully planned and masterminded by cons who explore weaknesses in the system and use them siphon money from unsuspecting investors.

Guarantee is the first RED FLAG that you need to be on the watch out for. When planning to invest in penny stocks, you will encounter marketers who seem to be so sure of how a penny stock will perform. Just like any other investment venture, stock investments have some degree of risks and uncertainties that nobody should accurately predicate including the firm selling its shares to the public. If you encounter a scenario where someone offering to sell you shares is certain of market trends, this could be a sign that the entire transaction has been stage managed which is tantamount to a scam.

Do not put your money in an unregistered product as this presents a serious risk for your investment. Actually, you should never proceed with the intention to buy penny stocks immediately you realize the product being offered is unregistered. What happens is these products are usually fronted by unlicensed individuals in order to escape scrutiny and detection from authorities. A majority of these unlicensed securities include stocks, bonds, notes and other bank investments. It is your responsibility to ensure that all transactions involving penny stock investments are thoroughly vetted before you put in your money and begin to trade.

Beware of stocks that experience consistent upward growth even when the market conditions are against a rise in the stock value. You need to understand that stock investments are volatile and therefore stock price increases and decrease are a norm. Remarkable and steady improvements when other stock prices are dwindling should make you suspicious. It is common knowledge that even the most successful and stable stocks suffer inconsistency on the market. As they always say, when a deal looks too good, you need to think twice.

As an investor, you have the right to know how your money is being spent and which type of investment ventures is the company undertaking to make money. Simplicity is critical particularly because investors get involved and are able to understand what is happening. You should keep off investments that are complex or shrouded in mystery. If professionals are managing your investment, they should come out clearly and explain to their investors in detail what they are engaged in and exercise the highest levels of transparency in all their dealings. You must know what you are putting your money into, what strategies have been put in place to ensure your investment grows as well as the challenges and risk affecting your penny stocks. This simply means that you need to ensure that you have understood all the critical details about your penny stocks before giving money to anyone.

Documentation is critical when purchasing penny stocks or any other type of investment. Whether you are investing in a stock, bond or mutual fund, proper documentation procedures need to be followed. You need to be furnished with all the required documentation that proves the authenticity of a security. Don't accept anyone to sell for you securities without the accompanying documentation – for instance if you have not been provided with a prospectus for stocks or mutual fund, you need to raise your eyebrows. For bonds, a circular duly signed by authorized persons need to be produced and the investor allowed to verify the documents. For the case of stocks, watching whether the stocks you intend to purchase have accompanying symbols or not is critical. In most cases, failure to produce documentation is a sign that the securities being sold have not yet been vetted and registered.

Inconsistency in your accounts is a serious matter that points to either a genuine mistake or a deliberate account to alter transactions. Penny stocks owners need to make sure that they regularly receive their account statements and thoroughly check them for any errors. If you point an error, you must within the shortest time possible bring it to the attention of the concerned persons. It also essential to check your statements and verify whether all the instructions you issued were followed.

Be sure to know who is responsible for your assets, in other words, you need to determine whether your investment adviser also doubles up as the custodian of your assets. This makes it easier to keep an eye on your account and know who to approach in case of a mistake. Experts advise that having an investment adviser as a custodian of your security is a better approach to safeguard your investment and easily detect fraud. If you use a third party custodian, you must make sure that all transactions associated with your account are above board.

Pushy salespeople can be annoying however this is not acceptable when it comes to penny stocks investment. When planning to invest, you need to be given time to carry out your own independent research and take time to make a decision. Professionalism demands that a salesperson should not push you into making a decision you have not carefully thought about. Aggressive salespeople are good for a company keen on strengthening their marketing tactics but should be treated with caution as some of them could be selling securities that are not legitimate or know that trading procedures are fraudulent. Forcing someone into a deal they have not thought about is not a good habit and also raises questions why a sales professional is in such a hurry to close the deal.

Having looked at the RED FLAGS that you need to avoid, it is time to be more alert and know when trouble is coming. A lot of penny stock investors have managed to detect scams thanks to being alert and simply knowing what is happening around them. You should not wait until it's too late to take action as chances of regaining your investment might be very slim or impossible.

Do not allow someone else to fully take control or manage an investment on your behalf without playing any oversight role. Investors continue suffering due to their ignorance and not playing a proactive role when it comes to monitoring their penny stocks. Don't allow yourself to be statistic of penny stock scams especially when you have access to information that can help safeguard you from these evils. There is a lot of information out there that you can use to make wise decisions and know when it's time to say no to a penny stock. If you don't know how to tell signs of fraud, you should find a professional and get advice on how you can trade in a secure environment that guarantees you the chance to maximize on your investment.

Playing safe and learning how to stay away from troubled stocks is the best way to ensure that you don't lose you hard earned money to cons who are keen to prey on innocent people who are only looking for a genuine way to secure their financial future.

Chapter Nine (Section a)

What Are Some of the Penny Stock Scams?

If you are planning to invest in penny stocks, it is a great idea to learn stock trading. Many investors have lost a lot of money in penny stock trading since they don't have the right information and steps necessary in stock trading. Although penny stocks are a great way to make quick money, you need to know that there are also risky because of many scammers. Talking to stock trading experts or broker can help you avoid getting scammed when trading stocks. In current economic times, there are different schemes that demand money from investors. This acts as an opportunity for new fraud and scammers look for any chance to exploit investors who wish to recover their losses.

Nowadays, Stock firms always issue alert to warn investors about common types of investment fraud and help investors to know and avoid types of tactics that scammers/fraudsters use. By carrying enough research on stock trading, you will be able find key red flags and equip yourself with tools that can help you to avoid penny stock scams. It is important to know that investment scams can take different forms and scammers are always on the look out to change their strategy. The most common penny stock scams are Pump and Dump and the Dump and Pump and stock list scams.

Pump and Dump and the Dump and Pump Penny stock scam

Pump and dump and the dump and pump are common penny stock scams which are created by marketers who work individually, micro -cap stock companies, broker and mafia in the attempt to make money off traders.

How does pump and dump scheme work?

Marketers who act as stock promoters buy large amounts of stocks from micro nap stock at very low prices. This kind of buying is done little at a time within weeks and months so as not to make the share prices trend too high. They do this to give stock the appearance of attracting investor interest. These stock promoters carry their responsibility of promoting thinly traded penny stocks or illegal existent stocks at high prices to investors thus causing the share process to increase from 10% to as much as 50% and even more.

Investors who are not keen see this as positive hyped marketing news about the stock and see trade activity and increased price as well as high volume of shares. This makes a lot of investors excited about penny stocks. In this type of penny stock scam, a naive investor will be controlled by the marketer stock promoter into thinking that the stock will go up as much as 300% or more. Such an investor will then buy shares of the stock hoping to get a lot of profits. Since the shares are usually affordable many investors are tricked by promoter to buy shares. This activity of many investors buying shares creates liquidity for marketers to sell shares at inflated prices. At the end, you as the investor end up facing losses contrary to profits once promised by marketers.

In penny stock scams, whether prices of shares fall or return to trading high again, it depends on a few factors such as nonexistent or fraudulent company, unnoticed good company and expertise of the marketer. Whether prices of shares plummet, and how far they plummet, or whether they eventually trade higher again depends on a number of factors, some of which are the following.

Many investors and traders who find themselves in penny stock scams must have bought shares of the stock at inflated prices. As the stock prices start dropping, some traders realize and sell their shares hoping to cap their losses. Other investors hold their shares long term hoping that they will go up in value again.

Dump and pump penny stock scam can backfire on a small company to fold the stock irreversible fall after the marketer scheme. This is a common risk that unnoticed good companies take when enlisting such advertising services. Many marketers benefit greatly from this kind of penny stock scam from payouts and from buying shares at low and later selling them at high prices after they are through promoting a company. It is good to know that many investors who purchased a penny stock scam lose their investment to the penny stock cam promoter and marketers.

In most cases, pump and dump penny stock scam are initially started by an actual scam company. The inside people of the particular company promote it with false news release that are hard to prove and use forward stock splits within a complicated marketer campaign. This done so as to create more shares so as to target a potential market cap for greater liquidity. This also gives false impression the shareholders are getting a reward for investing and that the company is doing well with great future returns. In turn this entices investors to buy more shares thus raising the share value.

The dump and pump penny stock scam is very similar to the promoter penny stock scam pump and dump. The promoter of dump and pump is known as a stock basher who turns into a stock promoter after the scam campaign achieves its purpose. This is the reason it is called "Dump and Pump". This scam has been in the penny stock market for a long period of time, yet many investors are not aware of how this scam works or how professionally organized it can be.

As an investor you need to know that some companies with a lot of debt but with great products in development also a major target of fraudsters. The American Stock Exchange (AMEX) is a common environment for the Pump and Dump and the Dump and Pump because many small listed struggling companies on the exchange. These small companies are regularly promoted by marketers that only promote exciting products. A lot of stock bashers monitor these stock promoting activities and leave after the share prices have peaked high enough.

Penny stocks listed on stock exchange are also prone to scammers. Instead of buying shares the stock basher sells shares of the stock before they begin the campaign of destruction on a struggling company. You should know that when shares sink, the stock bashers quickly buy back the shares they shorted for future profits. They start promoting them thus creates the Pump and Dump.

Being an inventor, you need to know the two major strategies the stock basher uses to benefit from demoting a stock. A stock basher always wishes to benefit by shorting stock shares and lowering prices down as traders sell their shares. Another strategy a stock basher use is buying back shares that they initially shorted after the share prices have gone too low. They help the shares recover by getting rid of positive marketing news.

When it comes to legality of penny stocks scams, it is unfortunate that most of these scams are conducted in a way to avoid legal problems. Although a company may have negative truthful information, this is not illegal.

How are Pump and Dump and the Dump and Pump promoted?

Over the years, the Pump and Dump and the Dump and Pump penny stocks scam has been promoted through cheap hot tips, cheap penny stock list, cheap hot stocks, stock listing services, free penny stock newsletters, free penny stock reports, penny stock robots, penny stock guru postings on stock focus headlines and message board posting by promoter and marketers pretending to be normal traders.

As an investor, you need to know that these kinds of free or cheap services are everywhere on the internet. The internet platform makes it easy for these scammers to reach the naive investors and take advantage of them. It is unfortunate that many season investors and traders become victims of such scams without realizing it. Penny stock trading experts warn one to refrain from investing in stocks that are being promoted. This is because many stocks are promoted by scammers.

Stock List Scams

Stock lists and stock picks are also common penny stocks scams. Stock lists are usually sent by newsletter and promoted on financial websites. If you want to try penny stock list, you need to be sure the source is reliable from a partner you trust. By conducting enough research on stock on the list before investing in any of them is encouraged. When it comes to hot penny stocks picks, many of them have been proved to be scams. Such stock picks are usually emailed to you after the stock has increased up by 25% or even more.

Penny stock list scams are always promoted on the internet. If you are investing ion penny stocks, it is a good idea to avoid using other company's stock lists because you are not sure if they are genuine stock lists and picks. It's better to have a general stock list of many genuine high potential stocks using specific instructions for choosing stocks. After you have developed the list, go through each of them over and over again until you come up with the best stocks.

It is important to know that many penny stocks are usually under $3.00 on the OTC and they need the help of marketer promotion. Marketer promotion is required because they help most investors recognize through media attention. As an investor, you should avoid buying stock on a penny list that has shot up with the promise that it will even go much higher. This does not happen and at the end you will be stuck holding shares at inflated prices.

Being an investor, you need to know how to spot extraordinary stocks that are target of marketer promoters. Once you invest in such stocks, they eventually explode in value on the marketer buying and promotions. After conducting enough research and investing in high potential stocks, you need to be patient. Don't be anxious if the stock you have invested does not explode in value the right or even id the stock goes down temporarily. You need to be confident in the research you carried out. Be confident that the stock you picked will trade well and go up thus make high profits.

When it comes to penny stocks scams it is important to train yourself to spot a penny stock scam. Remember to stay away from buying stocks on promotion that has increased in value with the promise of shares prices going much higher. Also you should look out for stocks that seem too good to be true. By researching on the company's history and its share prices is essential. As an investor, you should never invest on stock from a company before research on it. Research has helped many investors to learn about successful penny stock trading and know how to avoid penny stock scams.

Chapter Nine (Section b)

Boiler Room

Due to the tough financial economic times, for many people, income from employment or entrepreneurship is barely enough to cater for both short term and long term projects. Engagement in projects that demand huge finances have fuelled the need for borrowing of loans to be able to achieve personal goals such as buying a car, purchasing a home or even educating children. However, loans have to be repaid back at high interest rates within specified periods of time, this in turn exerts financial pressure on an individual. On the other hand, investing in ventures such as stocks has slowly become more popular and lucrative especially with the guaranteed return on investment particularly if proper ventures are identified.

The stock market has however suffered from a continuous streak of scams that have caused investors to lose billions of dollars. There are different types of scams that have rocked the industry in the past and recent years. Boiler rooms is a term well known in stock fraud referring to a scheme where investors are enticed to purchase stocks in a well-organized scheme that benefits insiders. In typical cases, investors get drawn by promises of the highest returns within the shortest time possible with the lowest levels of risks encountered.

When you examine closely, these deals usually seem too good to be true because promises given are usually unrealistic. Investment frauds have become common and now subscribe to various forms. Well planned and highly sophisticated schemes use enticement and pressure to lure unwitting investors to give out their money which is then defrauded. In most countries including the United States, share-related fraud schemes have had a serious economic impact on both investors and state economies.

Boiler Room Fraud has been defined by as the act of coercing investors to purchase certain stocks through marketing tactics such as cold calling. This fraud is also called 'share scams' and involves the sale of securities that have no value or worse off don't exist. Boiler rooms carry out their operations from call centers that are based abroad in order to avoid detection. The USA, Europe and Asia have particularly been associated with these call centers and use fake numbers and postal addresses to disguise themselves. Boiler rooms don't discriminate, they prey on both experienced and novice investors with an aim of duping them into investing in stock related scam deals. The consequences of boiler rooms have been felt far and wide with investors losing huge sums of money in deals that seemed quite clean and genuine.

Before you commit your finances to any type of investment, you should ensure you are absolutely sure about what you are about to purchase. The market has both real and genuine investment schemes as well as fraudulent ones. Investors need to take personal responsibility and research to identify the warning signs to prevent yourself from becoming a victim of scamming. The easiest way of making sure that you aren't conned is to check with SEC and other regulatory bodies for registered stock brokers and firms dealing with stocks. This is very important because in case anything goes wrong, you can be able to get assistance by lodging complaints with the SEC. Boiler rooms frauds can be avoided if you happen to spot the following suspicious signs:

Unsolicited calls and emails from abroad should spark suspicion. Be very careful when you receive information particularly from unknown persons from abroad convincing you to purchase certain stocks. Most of these phone calls usually promise high returns within a short period of time. The best way to avoid this is to hang up or just simply ignoring the phone calls, it is better not to give the callers time to sell for you these suspicious stocks.

Pressure to sell a stock is usually one of the most common signs of boiler rooms. Promoters of these stocks are usually quite convincing and insist a lot. Usually, they don't no for an answer and sometimes resort to threats and even become abusive especially when they realize you have refused their offer. Pressurized sales pitches are suspicious since a good marketer should give you the information and allow you to make a decision. Just make sure that you are not forced into buying stocks you have not adequately researched on.

Engaging in an investment is something you should be proud of to even discuss the achievement with your family or friends. However, you might come across opportunities where those selling for you the stocks ask you not to tell anybody and keep it a secret. If you are not allowed to brag about your stock investment, you should ask yourself why this is so. Some opportunities present themselves as "invitation-only "and are only for a selected few. You should stay away from secret investment ventures particularly from small companies you have no information about.

Boiler room frauds are known to ask their unsuspecting victims for their personal and financial information. Some of the issues you are likely to come across are frauds requesting you to pay upfront fees to act as deposits for a security or taxes. Private issues such as bank accounts, debit and credit cards should never be disclosed unless you are sure of the legitimacy of whoever is contacting you.

Check whether the people calling or contacting you have been registered by regulatory bodies such as SEC. Make sure that you only transact business with entities who have legally registered. If they are not, never engage in any business with them as this is a sign of a boiler room fraud.

Investors are encouraged to proceed with caution whenever they discover that a deal doesn't sound too good to be true. Many victims of boiler room scandals have been duped because of lack of sufficient knowledge and rushing to make decisions without carefully considering the consequences. It is for this reason that you need to research thorough and investigate any marketer that tries to sell for you stocks. Using the above pointers, you should be able to quickly pinpoint suspicious indications of an impending fraud.

The easiest way to stay away from boiler rooms is to be firm and not allowing anyone to pressure you into making investment decisions you are not sure about. One fundamental role for investment is you should never believe everything you are told. You need to ensure that any decisions regarding stock investments are clearly thought out and planned. Furthermore, if someone is marketing for you a particular stock, they should be in a position to tell you how the scheme works. On your part, you should clearly understand how an investment scheme works before putting your money into it. Business conducted between an investor and stock promoters should be defined by professional guidelines and fall within acceptable marketing strategies. Don't entertain stock promoters who are aggressive and become over friendly with the intention of securing your personal information. In other words, don't simply trust anyone particularly when it comes to your investment.

You don't have to say yes to every investment venture that comes your way. A good prospective investor must learn how to say no and stand firm by their word. If you are not comfortable with an investment idea, you shouldn't get into experiments. Wise investment calls for a sober mind and ability to make sound judgment for the best interest of your financial security. Stock scams have ruined many investors, as much as the authorities are doing all they can to detect them and apprehend suspects, you have a personal responsibility to watch out for boiler rooms and other share scams.

Chapter Nine (Section c)

What Type of Investments Do Boiler Room Operators Peddle?

These days, the urge to become financially independent has driven many people into considering investment as an option for gaining wealth. The current economic status and global financial meltdown has substantially increased the cost of living making impossible for one to use their traditional income earners to save for the future. In the past, investment was a preserve for the wealthy however this has changed in recent times as small scale investors come out to seek for ways to invest.

One concern however is the rising danger from several investment scams that have come up in the recent years. Every day, we get reports of investors who have lost thousands of dollars to cons who prey on unsuspecting victims with promises of handsome payouts within a short period of time. As an investor, you should be more careful and vigilant particularly when you decide to make any form of investment. Nowadays, scams are all over, so whether you are investing in stocks, real estate or any other venture, you need to protect yourself from greedy and unscrupulous con artists who want to make it big by exploiting you.

Boiler Room is probably one of the oldest scams that has successfully conned several thousands of investors across the world. As technology advances, this scam has been reinventing itself and come up with complex and clever methodologies used to entice victims to invest in worthless, non- existent and dubious investment schemes. As a matter of fact, the scope of this scam has increased and now targets investors putting their money in various projects across the board.

The main characteristic associated with Boiler Room is the fact that investors get contacted by convincing marketers through communication channels such as phone, email and fax with so-called lucrative investment offers. Remember, the trick boiler rooms use is to try and convince clients as much as possible to put their money into an investment project with the promise of high returns within limited time periods.

Every investor needs to be wary especially when planning to put their money into any type of project with the hope of attaining positive financial results. Boiler rooms are established in overseas countries and conduct their operations from remote location in order to escape detection from local regulatory bodies established to provide an oversight role. One important aspect to mention about Boiler Rooms is they cut across all types of investment. So, whether you are investing in stocks, bonds, forex, derivatives or physical assets, you need to be worried about the possibility of falling prey to Boiler Rooms scandals.

Anyone can be a victim of Boiler Room fraud. This is because people behind this scheme are not limited to any particular type of investment. If you are into stocks, bonds or real estate, you could become a victim. For these con artists, anyone who sees an opportunity to make some money from investment is a potential target. The tactics of these artists keep changing to ensure that they reap maximum benefits and go unnoticed. For instance, you don't have to invest in penny stocks to become their target, these guys are interested in every investor regardless of where you are planning to put your money.

Boiler Rooms have become very difficult to control because most of them conduct their operations from hidden locations abroad. This form of fraud is much more elaborate since it cuts across several investment types. Perpetrators and insiders working with Boiler Rooms understand that their business can only thrive if they devise ways to con investors across the board. Unlike fraud schemes such as pump and dump that are limited to stocks, boiler rooms have a larger audience and make use of this advantage to rake in millions of money from investors around the world.

A boiler room is well managed and its activities carried out by professionals who have a clear understanding of their target market, products and what they need to do to convince new clients to sign up with them. Here, a wide variety of professionals who understand how various securities and investment operate use their industry knowledge and tactics to look for loopholes and opportunities to exploit for selfish gains.

A lot of cases involving boiler rooms scandals have been reported and are under investigation. One distinct observation is that you will realize these scandals take different angles. There are complains of investors who have been conned from stock investments, others have lost money by investing in bonds while another group of investors suffered losses trying to invest in physical assets. Boiler Room scandals are not after a certain group of investors, they are conclusive and interested in anyone willing to part with their money for investment purposes. For this reason, quite a number of victims across the globe have fallen prey to this scam.

The good news is that there are places conned investors can seek help in case they have fallen victim to Boiler Room fraud. It is important for you to learn the warning signs of this fraud so that you can take appropriate measures to protect yourself. A lot of governments are doing all they can to ensure that they work hand in hand to reign in on Boiler Rooms that are operating from foreign lands. The scandal has definitely caused ripples in the industry particularly because investors now feel that they are not safe.

The most important thing to do is to act with caution and avoid being forced or coerced into an investment you have not thought about and researched. Boiler Rooms use the language of enticing, intimidation and promises of unrealistic returns. The power to make decisions lies with you and you have the right to reject an offer in totality particularly if you feel skeptical. A number of perpetrators of these scams have been arrested and convicted but the problem is so deeply rooted to the extent that it cannot be solved at once.

The signs of Boiler Rooms have now become pretty obvious yet it's unfortunate some people are still getting conned even with plenty of information around to safeguard investors from con artists. Fraud perpetrators are peddling varied ventures with an aim of capturing the attention of people looking for somewhere to invest their cash. Some investors have become victims of Boiler Room scams as result of metal and jewelry trading. This shows how deeply rooted the fraud has affected the industry. Fighting such a scam demands a lot of effort considering some of the people involved are policy makers who intentionally exploit weak links in the system to commit crime. Operators of this scam have skillfully learnt the art of human psychology and employ all manner of tricks to ensure that you give into their demands.

The best way to handle these promoters is to cease any form of communication with them particularly if you are suspicious about the deal being promoted. Cutting off communication sends signals to the fraudsters that you are not interested in whatever they have to market. However, engaging with them for a long time gives them time to study your personality and scheme a plan on how to ensure you fall prey to their tricks. As an investor, you need to be firm particularly when you are discussing investment deals with anybody, becoming too friendly and blindly agreeing to everything being said makes you vulnerable and con artists would want to use this advantage to milk you dry.

Chapter Nine (Section d)

Internet Fraud – Pump and Dump

The stock market has recently become one of the most sought after investment ventures particularly for investors willing to expand their financial assets. The recent past has seen an increase in the number of people researching for available opportunities in this industry. Tremendous success has been associated with investing on the stock market, on the flip side however is an increasingly worrying trend of increased cases of fraud in the sector. The success associated with the industry has also attracted greedy and unscrupulous industry players engaged in trading multi-practice that upsets stock prices with an aim of gaining maximum profits at the expense of the investors.

Penny stocks are very attractive because they cost relatively less to invest in. However, these stocks have suffered major setbacks particularly due to various scams that have caused investors to lose their money. If you are interested to invest in penny stocks, it's a wise idea to research about scams that have affected the industry and how you can safeguard your investment.

The Pump and Dump scam has been responsible for the loss of revenue for many investors dealing with penny stocks. Quite a number of con scheme exist in the industry but this particular one has caused major upsets prompting high scale investigations to establish the loopholes that cons could be using to execute the scam. When you visit the internet, you will find a lot of information on pump and dump scams. It is important to learn about this scam, how it is executed and how it can affect your investment. It's of paramount importance to educate yourself well in advance before making any financial commitments. Scammers use this fraud scheme as an opportunity to use unethical techniques to manipulate the markets for their own benefit.

What is Pump and Dump scam?

This happens when marketers working in conjunction with other key industry players such as penny stock companies and brokers engage in unacceptable schemes in order to make money off others in the trading chain. What many of you may not know is we also have Dump and Pump which is not discussed so much as Pump and Dump, the tactics used are basically the same.

This scheme is usually executed so well that investors never have the slightest idea of what is going on. For an investor, the venture looks perfect and lucrative on the outside. This scam involved organized, well planned and coordinated schemes that take place behind the scenes. Actually, it's impossible to get wind of them unless you are an insider with access to confidential details about stock trading practices.

In order understand the scam better, we need to learn how Pump and Dump is orchestrated and who is involved in the scheme. The people in charge of promoting particular stocks (marketeers) usually begin purchasing selected stocks at negligible bottom prices. This stock purchasing is usually done over a period of time to allow an increase in stock prices and portray to the outside market an increasing level of investor interest. In most cases, the stock marketed is usually genuinely good and promising but promoters use a thinly traded or non-existent stock to advertise it with exaggerated prices sometimes as high as 4 times the real value.

When this happens, investors witness the positive hype associated with a stock accompanied with a stock price increase and substantial volume of stocks traded. As a result, anyone willing to invest in that particular stock becomes excited and sees it as a good stock. Naïve traders are usually made to believe that positive trading around the stocks will further the prices as high as 200% or even more. The optimistic news associated with the stock is then forms the basis of traders purchasing the stock with the hope of making profits.

Increased purchasing makes the thinly or non- existent stocks to skyrocket in price way past the inflated price. Remember that the sharp price increase is not because there are plenty of enough sellers to comfortably match up with buy orders which should be the case. When stocks are bought at a high rate, marketeers now get a perfect opportunity to benefit from increased liquidity as a result of increased volume trading activity as well as increased market cap. Liquidity in this case implies the number of buyers is enough to meet the needs of those who are intending to sell off their stocks at similar prices.

Stock promoters then collude with other industry players to begin the sale of stocks when there are a huge number of traders available to buy them. This continues as long as traders continue to purchase the stock causing some small ripples in the share prices. When this happens, the rise in stock prices reduces momentum with promoters coming out to assure new investors that this is the best time to invest or existing shareholders increase their shares before the stocks resume a steady upward trend.

At some point in the trading, marketeers then decide to dump the remaining stocks they owned causing the markets to react with prices plummeting to very low levels almost to the same point they were earlier before they bought them. This process happens in a number of cycles causing the share prices to ultimate between very high and low prices. it is important to note that for Pump and Dump scam, the price at which these shares trade depend on factors discussed below:

- If it was a fraudulent company or a non-existent stock that was promoted, there comes a time when it is discovered to be a sham and perpetrators of this scheme are forced to dump their shares.

- Good companies that could have performed well even if media announcements were used. Such a stock is likely to continue trading at good prices. Some stocks continue performing well even after the hype created is long gone because of their great affinity for exponential growth.
- The marketeer's skill to promote stock to a particular level in order to achieve the desired results.

What happens in this scam is investors purchase stocks at already inflated prices. When prices begin to drop, some traders engage in frantic efforts to dispose their stocks with a hope of capping their losses. On the other hand, some hold onto the stocks longer anticipating the shares prices to increase thanks to market hype that reassures investors that the current price dips are only temporary. There are also those who continue purchasing these stocks at low prices that contributes to the swing in prices.

Consequences of a Pump and Dump Scam

Penny stock scams benefit marketeers who are engaged in manipulation of the markets in order to sway stock prices to levels that will suit them. In most cases, they benefit from handsome payouts from firms that hire them as well as buying shares at lows and disposing them at unbelievably high prices after thoroughly promoting the stocks.

On the other hand, investors who bought these scam stocks or were duped into the scheme end up losing huge amounts of their investments to penny stock scam promoters and insiders. Pump and Dump has caused many people to lose their hard earned money to a few individuals who make use of their insider knowledge to achieve personal selfish gains.

In summary, a penny stock scam particularly Pump and Dump begins either with a genuine or scam company. The stock promoters then work on a strategy to create hype about the stock to elicit public interest. This is done by releasing fake press releases, news statements which are impossible to prove their authenticity. The theory of forward stock splits is then used accompanied with a vigorous and complex marketer campaign to manipulate the prices.

The reason why all this is done is to find ways of creating more shares available for purchase creating leeway for higher liquidity as well as a greater potential market cap. Shareholders and new investors are also duped to anticipate great rewards in response to the positive trading patterns that ultimately hope to substantially increase the value of the stock. Investors are usually promised good future returns if they buy the shares and stock with them for longer periods. Strategies are usually formulated to entice shareholders to increase their volume of shares thus causing the share price to witness an increase in share price. Scam artists then formulate ways of fleecing shareholders before dumping the shares.

This scam is usually well planned and involves a professional network of industry players who understand the market quite well. They find loopholes to exploit and begin fleecing investor's money covering up their trade so well that it becomes impossible to notice their fraudulent activities. Since Pump and Dump was discovered, many investors have lost trillions of dollars to these schemes that seem to be evolving everyday with new tactics making them very difficult to expose. As a penny stock investor, it is wise to understand how this and other scams operate before investing your money in stocks. Using this information, you can also be able to make wise and informed decisions.

The internet has helped stock investors to achieve high levels of independence when it comes to stock trading. The possibility of monitoring your own stocks using online platforms has now become a reality. However, scammers have also found clever ways of manipulating online stock trading platforms to extort money from unsuspecting investors. The high level of risk associated with penny stocks makes them quite volatile. Be sure to discuss these issues with a reputable stock broker who can also advise you on how to invest wisely and safely.

Chapter Nine (Section e)

Where Can I Turn To For Help If I Become the Subject of a Penny Stock Fraud?

Trading penny stocks has become very common today. May investors have admitted investing a lot of money in stock trading so as to make huge profits. What you need to know as an investor is that penny stock trading is very risky. Although you can make many from stock trading, you also need to know that you can lose a lot of money. Engaging in stock trading without carrying out proper research can lead to losing money. It is important to know that there a lot of stock listing on the internet that you can use though not all of them are genuine. This is why many stock trading experts advise investors and traders to explore each stock listing carefully so as to come up with genuine and legit companies. Penny stock being a great platform to make money, it has also become a ground for scammer and fraudsters. Many investors have reported losing huge sums of money to penny stocks scams.

The amazing thing is that many investors and traders who become victims of scammers for not release there being scammed. This is because many penny stock fraudsters are so good at their game and run scam campaign in a professional way that it's hard to tell it's a scam. Being an investor, you need to know the red flags of penny stock scams and be able to identify major penny stock scams. In case you find yourself a victim of penny stock fraud, you need to know that you can ask for help. Many traders and investors who have been scammed have been able to report penny stock scams hence not only helping themselves but also other traders.

One of the places where you can turn to for help if you become the subject of a Penny Stock Fraud is FINRA. FINRA which stands for Financial Industry Regulatory Authority is a dedicated to have investor protection and market integrity through effective and efficient regulation of the securities industry. You can file a complaint through an online complaint form or print the form and fax or mail to the offices. However, you need to know that there is no assurance that any action taken by FINRA will lead to payment or return of funds or securities.

 Financial Fraud Enforcement Task Force is a great platform to report penny stock fraud to get help. This establishment helps to fight financial fraud by helping in investigating, prosecuting financial crimes as well as ensuring just and effective punishment to those who partake in stock fraud. The organization has more than 20 Federal Agencies, 90 Attorneys offices, state and local partners. It is one of the best firms that help to combat fraud. Once you submit your case, an attorney will carry n investigations and find the best way to help you.

Last but not least, you can talk to an investment expert to guide you through the process of getting help if you are a subject of penny stock fraud. With the help of their advice, you will be able to find the best guidance on how to go about the process.

Chapter Nine Section f)

How Do I Protect Myself from Internet Fraud?

If you wish to make it in the penny stock trading, you need to learn the right skills for stock trading. Finding an honest, experienced and qualified broker to help you out when it comes to penny stock trading is very important. A good broker should invest in the client's funds by putting their client's first even if the market brings bad result. However, some clients end up losing money due to dishonest from brokers. Over a long period of time of many clients investing in stocks have been victim of fraud. Good news, many stock trading companies, brokers and firms have come up with helpful information that investors can use to protect themselves from fraud.

One of the best ways that you can do to protect yourself from internet fraud during stock trading is to investigate your stock broker before using them. Prior opening an account you need to take time when selecting a broker. It is always a great idea to ask a trusted friend for referral that they trust. As an investor, you need to avoid taking cold calls from brokers you don't know. A broker who is focused on making money may not help you. Visiting the broker's office, checking their education background, experience in stock trading and investment formula is encouraged. Look out for a broker who is not willing to know you in person or answer your questions. Remember to do a background check to find out if the stockbroker has any negative history, feedback or criminal convictions.

Having your broker know about your objectives in stock trading is also a great way to stay away from fraud. Letting your broker know about how much you are willing to spend or risk is important. Writing a detailed letter of confirmation to the particular broker with another copy to the office manage is good idea. This way, your intentions will be understood and clear.

When it comes to stock trading, if the deal seems too good to be true then it is. No matter what your broker says you need to know that the higher investment returns always lead higher risks. If you don't understand an investment, it is good to avoid it. Always look out for suspicious projections based past performance. Trusting optimistic stock projections that don't look real is dangerous and you could lose a lot of money.

Taking time reading everything is also important. As an investor it is good idea to take time ti read through documents presents before putting your signature. Reading through a document will help you to confirm if the information and data is accurate and within your investment objective. In case you don't understand anything, ask help from an expert. At this point, you also need to review confirmation account statements and slips carefully. By chance you notice something you can't comprehend, call your broker.

As a stock investor, your broker has no right to sell or buy stocks without consulting you first. Giving a broker complete right to trade your account is very risky as well as letting him write checks on your bank account and using your charge cards. If you happen to find trade in your account that you didn't authorize, you need to follow it up immediately by writing a certified letter to your branch manager and revoke the authorized trade. A broker trading your account without your permission is against the law and a theft.

You also need to know how a broker should be paid. In most cases, a broker is paid on commission basis by buying and selling securities in your account. Whether you make profits or losses, a broker has to be paid their commission. Stock brokers purchase and sell stocks in a regular basis so as to make income.

Learning and understanding loads and other fees in stock trading is essential. It is good to know that high commissions do not necessary equate to high quality. In real sense, the higher the commission for a product the greater the return the investment must make to be even. You need to avoid getting into stock trading and paying fees that you don't understand. Instead of making money, you could end up spending all your investment in unrealistic fees that do not add up.

As much as possible, you also need to avoid margins so at to reduce your chances of getting into internet fraud. Margin trading leads to higher commissions for the stockbroker which exposes you to higher risk. When you decide to trade on margin, you are simply borrowing money from a brokerage firm so as to buy more securities thus more commissions. The collateral you put for the loan from the brokerage firm acts as the security you have in your account. If the price for the securities goes low, you will get into a margin call which requires you to sell your stocks or put more money into your account. If you purchase stocks on margin and they decrease in price, you can even lose your investment and in turn own a lot of money to the brokerage firm.

In case you mess up in stock trading, you should not be afraid or feel embarrassment. Most of the time, investors who have been abused in stock trading always win back their losses and get interest, lawyer's fees and damages from their brokers in arbitration cases. However, you want to go this way you need to act quickly because there are limits for asking for claims. If you realize that you have been victimized, you need to contact experienced arbitration attorney at once.

Again, to protect to yourself form internet fraud in stock trading, you need to educate yourself. Investing in materials that will help you to learn about stock trading is encouraged. The internet has a lot of information that you can read thus help you to stay away from fraud in stock trading. You need to know that as an investor, information and education is the best tool you can have to protect your future and investment.

Asking for questions from stock experts is a great idea. A good broker should also be in a position to educate you on how to protect your money so as not to be a victim of fraud. The Securities and Exchange Commission (SEC) is committed to protecting investors and has great information on safe stock trading.

Last but not least, you need to check out investment professionals. It is a great idea to ask the promoter of the investment opportunity is licensed to sell your investment. Remember to confirm which regulator issued the promoter the license and when the license has been suspended. A certified securities marketer or promoter should be licensed and his firm must also be registered with FINRA, SEC or state securities regulator.

These are some of the things you can do so as to protect yourself from internet fraud. Others can be found on the internet or other helpful stock trading materials. As an investor, you need to know that by using this helpful information, you will not only be protecting your investment but also your future.

Chapter Nine (Section g)

What Do I Do If I Suspect that something is Amiss After I have made a Penny Stock Investment?

You only feel comfortable when you are assured that your investment is safe and sound. In recent times, the stock market industry has become very lucrative for investors keen on growing their financial fortunes. On the flip side, the increased demand for penny stock investment has attracted professional con artists taking advantage of the investment upsurge to swindle investors of their hard earned cash. Before making any bold financial moves, it's always advisable to research thoroughly and carefully consider all the available options before making any decisions.

It's heartbreaking to invest in something that eventually goes down the drain. The conscience plays a big role in our lives and therefore you should pay attention to observations or feelings about something. When you get a feeling that something isn't right, you need to move back and revaluate your strategy and decisions. Some of us get excited and plunge ourselves into penny stock investments that later turn out to be fake. Lack of adequate research and engaging the right caliber of professionals can seriously jeopardize your chances of making any substantial returns from penny stocks.

However, in an industry that has been lately associated with several high level scams, you might get surprised when you find out your investment could have landed into a fraudulent scheme. When this happens, it's time to quickly find solutions before it's too late. A lot of investors wait too long to take any meaningful action even after learning that their investment is at great risk. An investment that is real could later turn out to be suspicious particularly because of the nature of transactions involving the penny stock. Wise investors know too well the consequences of gambling their life savings in an investment that is doomed to fail.

The immediate action that you can consider is to liquidate all your stocks and quit the investment plan. This however will depend on the nature of the price as well as the level of losses or potential risk facing the stocks. If you still have a good chance of recouping your funds, its better not to hesitate as suspicious dealings in a stock can have dire consequences within a split second. Don't wait for cons to prey on your investment as you simply sit back and watch, suspicious cases of penny trading should immediately trigger a series of instant actions to safeguard your investment.

Unfortunately, many cases of penny stock suspicious dealings don't get reported because several companies dealing with penny stocks have are not answerable to any regulatory authority. Companies with less than $10million turnover are not covered by SEC oversight role of ensuring that trade execution procedures are conduced ethically and in accordance to industry standards. Cons take advantage of these pitfalls in the system to create a perfect environment for committing their crimes and in most cases, getting away undetected. This however doesn't mean that you cannot make an official complaint regarding suspicious trading activities.

Fortunately, there are legal procedures that can apply particularly if some industry players are breaking the rules. Some scams however get to the inside of a courtroom and victims can get a fair hearing to determine the outcome of the cases. If you realize that a company is posting incorrect information on public message boards, you need to take quick action and report this to a top government agency. If the companies you invest in report to a regulatory body, it's a good idea to lodge a formal complaint with the concerned authorities to pave way for investigations. Unlawful acts that need to be reported include abuse of chat rooms, posting incorrect information in financial articles or any other media used by the public to get information.

Government authorities in charge of the stock market have the right to reprimand and demand for answers whenever they come across industry players committing various forms of violation. Bashers who issue false financial reports and statements that in the long run jeopardize the price of a security should be reported for disciplinary action to be taken against them.

Scam artists who misuse financial message boards are breaking the law and need to be held accountable for their actions. Financial message boards have their TOS (Terms of Service) that clearly outline the rules that members need to abide to. Established message boards have put in place mechanisms and facilities that allow reporting of TOS violations. In the recent past, viewers using the boards have been empowered using facilities such as chat to inform administrators about any unscrupulous and suspicious trading activities.

As an investor, you need to understand the implications of tolerating the vice of suspicious trading transactions and how they can affect your investment. Message board service providers may at times not be vigilant enough to detect vices within their systems. Different discipline approaches have been adopted by board administrators to ensure that anyone caught engaging in any form of malpractice is punished. Some of the measures taken include writing a letter of warning to the violator, removing posts that don't confine to the rules of the boards. More radical measures such as temporary or permanent ban of violators as well as instituting legal proceedings are options taken particularly for repeat violators.

It is your responsibility as an investor to ensure that all those engaged in trading malpractices are not allowed escape disciplinary measures. Since there are channels available for seeking legal redress, it is important for investors to make use of them and ensure that bad eggs in the penny stock business are exposed and punished. Before purchasing penny stocks, you need to do your research and establish whether there are any options to report suspected violations. This is very important because you have the right to monitor your investment and ensure that cons don't get a chance to enrich themselves with your fortune. A good stock should empower its investors to complain and seek action for perpetrators of scams.

Chapter Nine (Section h)

How to Initiate a Loss Recovery

We all make investments for the sake of getting extra cash either to finance large scale projects or save for the future. The number of investors considering stock investment as a way of securing their financial future has become high. It is important to note that any type of investment comes with its own risks therefore the possibility of a loss occurring and how to recover from it is information you need to have prior making an investment. A loss occurs when a security posts a lesser price than the initial investment amount put down by the investor.

Suffering loss from an investment can be very devastating particularly due to the fact that a lot of money is lost in the process. Having a documented roadmap of how loss can be mitigated is crucial information for anyone willing to participate in an investment venture. There are several possibilities that lead to loss in an investment, while some factors may be purely due to fluctuation and volatility of market conditions, others may be caused by deliberate intention orchestrated through various types of investment frauds and schemes. In some cases, there are opportunities to either fully or partially recover money put into an investment depending on the underlying circumstances leading to the loss.

When putting your money in stocks or any other investment venture, you should research, talk to experts in order to clearly understand what action steps can be taken in the event of a loss. Depending on the nature of the investment and what caused the loss, it could be impossible to initiate any loss recovery method that will bear any fruits. For instance, victims of Boiler Room fraud unfortunately lose all their money because this fraud is usually perpetrated from abroad making it difficult for local oversight bodies to launch investigations and prosecute those who are found to be guilty.

For a fraud, the first step to make is to report the case to the relevant authority concerned with investing investment scams. It is always important to keep as much documentation as possible when you are a member of an investment club as this information can later be useful for the purposes of investigation. Any emails, faxes and even recorded phone call conversations can act as good evidence to begin an investigation into a suspected fraud scheme. Remember, when you intend to initiate a loss recovery due to fraud, you must have sufficient evidence to sustain your case as well as facilitate investigators to do their work.

Recovering money should be the main agenda for seeking justice in case you have fallen victim of a fraud investment scam. It is good to note that you can report to the police or bodies charged with the responsibility of investigating fraud cases. In case you have lost huge sums of money, you should consider file for civil recovery proceedings. The best way to increase your chances of loss recovery is to act immediately you discover you are a victim of fraud. It is crucial to make a formal compliant as early as possible because it significantly increases the chances of getting assisted to recover your money.

Many investment fraud victims lose their money because they take too long to act which further jeopardizes their chances of recovering lost money. When you research on the internet, you will also come across various loss recovery mechanisms you can use to get justice and possibly recoup some of your investment. In many cases, victims usually fail to get the full amount that was put into the project but there's a possibility of getting back some percentage of the initial investment capital.

The presence of security arbitration experts has come as a huge sigh of relief particularly for victims of loss incurred as a result of investment. The increased number of cases related to fraud and investments gone sour has led to the introduction of professional firms whose mandate is to ensure that victims get justice and compensation whenever they incur losses as a result of investing their money in various ventures.

Investment recovery professionals have successfully assisted investors to seek justice through legal proceedings to reduce the level of losses incurred from investing. These firms target clients who have suffered losses in areas such as the stock market as well as other ventures. Aside from fraud, you could lose your money because of carelessness and professional misconduct of your stock broker. If your broker fails to have your best interests in mind, chances are high that they could end up engaging in trade transactions that could prove risky for your fortune. Investigations carried out by these professionals seek to determine whether you were misled to buy the investment without the seller sufficiently explaining the level of risk involved.

Any loss recovery investigation begins by first determining whether the correct procedures were followed at the time you were making the purchase. Stock brokers involved are also investigated to establish whether they adequately played their role to help you understand the safety of your investment or they simply didn't follow the instructions you had issued. As earlier indicated, some of these issues might not necessarily imply there were fraudulent activities taking place at the time and period of investment.

The advantage of using investment recovery firms to get your money back is the fact that they have handled several similar cases in the past and are therefore in a good position to offer helpful professional advice and expertise. The good news is that most of these firms are ready to provide you with affordable representation to ensure that as an abused investor, you find a platform to help you recover your funds through processes such as negotiation and securities arbitration. With thorough knowledge in securities, investment recovery professionals help you to recover stock market losses that could have been caused by investment fraud, stock broker fraud or professional misconduct.

The good thing about this service is that most of them offer free consultation and will readily review your case at no cost. If the investigations reveal that there is a increased likelihood of recovering your money, investment recovery firms always begin a vigorous process aimed at achieving this. In such cases, payment is only made when you have successfully recovered your money.

These companies have a defined approach and methodology used to determine whether an investment was suitable for you or not. The main focus here is to check whether the investment recommendation was ideal at the time it was sold to an investor. Here, it is essential to know whether the client understood the risk associated with the investment and were they ready to take the risk. Issues of whether the customer could afford the risk or not are also looked into just be sure that the correct decisions were made at the time a client was signing up for an investment.

All the above mentioned issues need to in the affirmative to rule whether the recommendation was above board or not. It is through such case studies that investigators get to discover fraud or misconduct and provide further advice on how to deal with the loss recovery. It is a painful experience to lose money in regardless of whether it's fraud, negligence and misconduct. Using investment recovery firms to initiate loss recovery has helped many people to successfully win compensation. These firms are mostly run by attorneys and therefore their operations are well within the legal confines, approaching them is the best way to seek legal redress if you feel cheated.

Book Review Request

Thank you for reading my book Understanding Penny Stock Investment, Book 3 for Teens and Young Adults. If you ever have a spare moment, it would be a great help if you could post a review of it on Amazon and let other potential readers know why you liked it. It's not necessary to write a lengthy, formal review—a summary of the comments from you would be perfectly fine. Here's a link to the review form for my book:

About the Author

Ronald E. Hudkins (1951-Present) was born in Canton, Ohio and grew up in Massillon, Ohio. He was drafted into military service in 1970 where he remained up until 1993 when he retired honorably from the U.S. Army, Military Police Corps. During his service and after, he attended many universities that include Kent State University, Maryland University, Central Texas College (European Branch), Blair Junior College, Hagerstown Junior College and Phoenix University. He mostly completed general studies but declared two majors in the areas of both Business Administration and a Bachelor of Science in Information Technology.

Ronald Hudkins as of August 2014 has published twelve books in both the fiction and nonfiction categories across many genres. Please feel free to review his works on his author's website at RonaldHudkins.com

Author's Other Books

Nonfiction

Dec 26, 2013

Ronald E. Hudkins

Aug 12, 2014

Aug 22, 2014

Mar 7, 2017

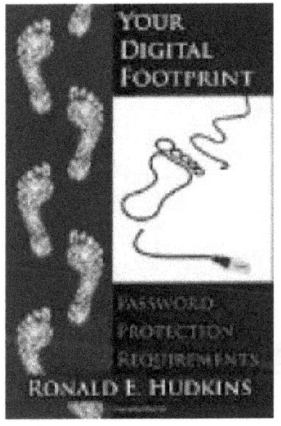

Jun 12, 2014

Jul 12, 2007

Fiction

Dec 21, 2013

Mar 20, 2013

Nov 16, 2013

Pending

Mar 19, 2014

May 10, 2014

See the above listed books wholesale and retail outlets at the following site;

RONALDHUDKINS.COM

The Author's Books are generally available in the following formats;

V	Medium Options	V
Android	Desktop	Tablet
eReader	Windows	IOS
	Smartphone	
Audio	Paperback	ePub
	^ Format Options ^	

Internet Presence Ronald Hudkins

My Other Projects page is where friends and followers of the author Ronald E. Hudkins and publisher of the book Senior Things I Said, Say, Did and Do Volume One can see the authors other Internet activities.

Business Sites on the Internet

The Healthy Living Mall

Ever just want a one source stop for Diet and Weight loss, Exercise and Fitness, Mental Health, Men's Health, Nutrition and Women's Health? That storefront is now here! Visit **http://digijunction.com/health/guard1**

What is The Healthy Living Mall?

The healthy living mall is unlike any other place you have visited before. I am sure you care about your health more than anyone else in the world and the healthy living mall is the one place that can help you. The healthy living mall is like a library that has the knowledge, expertise, and experience to help you achieve your health goals.

Do not worry about what your overall goal is because the healthy living mall has what you need. Some of you may have a goal to lose weight or improve fitness. Some of you may even be trying to focus on one specific aspect on your health.

These are all noble goals and this site can help you achieve any of them that you chose to work on.

Now you do not have to have a goal to work out every day or get ripped. Part of why this site is here for everyone is because it helps people work with conventional treatments as well as other non-traditional methods. Some people prefer more natural and alternative medicines which work just as well. The healthy living mall gives you this power over your health and gives you the knowledge to make these important decisions.

The way this site works is by breaking down all your possible needs into different sections. This makes it much easier for you to navigate your way through and easily find everything you need. All the information here is free for you so be sure to take advantage of it whenever you want.

The Health Mall is constantly being updated with the newest and latest health information. You should go ahead and save this page to your favorites and your bookmarks. This way you can easily get here again later. So, check us out at **http://digijunction.com/health/guard1**

Home Business Resource Center

If there is anything you need to know about Affiliate Marketing, Auctions, Classified Ads, Consulting, Home Employment, Internet Marketing, Paid Surveys or Software this is your home business resource, training and most up to date news information available to date on the Internet! Visit;**http://digijunction.com/business/guard1**

About the ultimate Home Business Resource Center.

Maybe you are looking for a little extra cash. Or maybe you'd like to tell your boss that he can "take your job and give it to some other sucker". Whatever your reason for looking for a new home based business you've come to the right place.

With all the scams and downright bogus products out there it can be hard to decipher the legitimate opportunities from the duds. Well, we've made it extremely easy for you by providing you with access to the very best programs in the entire home based business categories. Look at this site as your perfect one stop shop for finding your perfect home business.

Perhaps you are looking for a home business that can replace a full time income or even produce a six or seven figure income. While some of you might be looking to pocket an extra few hundred to a few thousand dollars in your spare time. Whichever category you fall under this site will have the perfect business for you.

This site is broken down into several categories to help you find what is right for you. Whether you are a beginner or a seasoned pro you'll be sure to find the perfect home business here.

So go ahead, look around and find the home business that is right for you.

Also, please be sure to bookmark this site as we make updates with the newest and hottest programs often.

http://digijunction.com/business/guard1

Investing for Profit

If you are looking for some of the very best investment programs and services relative to Commodities, Forex, Options, Personal Finance, Real Estate and Stocks this site has you covered. Remember, the right knowledge can mean the difference between significant gains and catastrophic losses. We're here to give you the right knowledge for each market. Visit;
http://digijunction.com/investing/guard1

About Investing for Profit

If you are guessing or simply do not know what you are doing in the world of investment you can lose a lot of your hard earned money. Sure, you can get lucky and actually establish some profitable investments but you can also see your profits get wiped out in an instant. However with the proper guidance, tools and self help education you can learn to limit any losses in any market and this site is designed specifically to show you how.

Here at the Investing for Profit digital mall you will find the absolute top of the line investment programs and service that are currently or about to be available. It does not matter where you interests are held be it in Stocks, FOREX, options, real estate or stocks this site will keep you investing intelligently. You know as well as I the difference between exceptional gains or disastrous losses boils down to just having the correct knowledge. At this site you have the complete and correct knowledge no matter which market you invest in.

One of the best things about the Investing for Profit Mall is the selection of programs that are available. Different sectors and trading styles can be hot at various times. When there is a bull market in natural gas, gold or oil you can check out the many featured programs in the commodities trading area. If the stock market is sinking maybe with more investment option programs is right for you. This site allows you to educate yourself completely for whatever market you choose to place your investments.

So go ahead, look around and find the investing strategies that are right for you. Also, please be sure to bookmark this site as we make updates with the newest and hottest programs often.

http://digijunction.com/investing/guard1

StoreDoor

StoreDoor is a place where the mugs are just a little bit different. Perhaps a bit bitter/sweet for the person looking for a slightly different (not so tactful) way to express a crude feeling about a person, place, thing or event.

http://www.zazzle.com/storedoor

Member Social Sites

Delicious.com (Article Postings)

http://www.delicious.com/stacks/view/EkApbc

Stumbpleupon.com

http://www.stumbleupon.com/stumbler/ron29950

Digg.com (Article Postings)

http://digg.com/settings/links

YouTube

http://www.youtube.com/user/rh112131

Pinterest

http://www.pinterest.com/rhudkins/

Facebook (Follow Me!)

https://www.facebook.com/ronald.hudkins

Twitter

https://twitter.com/HudkinsR

Figment

http://figment.com/users/361031-Ronald-E-Hudkins

Wattpad

http://www.wattpad.com/user/rhudkinsv

Goodreads

https://www.goodreads.com/user/show/15853675-ronald-hudkins

Amazon Page

http://www.amazon.com/-/e/B00ATQ83JA

Shelfari

http://www.shelfari.com/ronaldhudkins

Linkedin

http://www.linkedin.com/pub/ronald-hudkins/4a/356/749

Smashwords

https://www.smashwords.com/profile/view/rhudkins **ask David**

http://askdavid.com/books/7702

Public Bio's

Expert Author Bio on EzineArticles

http://ezinearticles.com/?expert=Ronald_Hudkins

Linkedin.com (Business Profile Page)

http://www.linkedin.com/pub/ronald-hudkins/4a/356/749

MarketerProfiles.com (by Charlie Page)

http://www.marketerprofiles.com/?a=h&c=&mode=&p=4

Blog Spots on the Internet

SelfGrowth.com

http://www.selfgrowth.com/experts/ronald_hudkins.html

Slide Shows

Slide Presentations -
http://www.slideshare.net/hudkinsr

Author Stream - Video Presentations

http://www.authorstream.com/Presentation/aSGuest130361-1369066-10-slightly-different-ways-to-advertise/

Thank You!!!!

Lightning Source UK Ltd.
Milton Keynes UK
UKHW02f1849150218

317967UK00006B/268/P

9 781500 916282